ADVANCE PRAISE FOR *BUSTING THE REAL ESTATE INVESTING LIES*

"*Kim and Jimmy are talented entrepreneurs, each committed to growing the value they create 10x. Here, they collaborate to provide those seeking financial freedom with a game-changing real estate investing capability, starting with a new mindset. This is an example of the best of what entrepreneurs do to create a bigger financial future for others.*"

—Dan Sullivan, founder of Strategic Coach®

"*If you are behind on your retirement planning, this book will show you how to get back on track in a hurry—while reducing your risk! Proven strategies for real wealth by two people who practice what they preach. Kim and Jimmy are experts in their respective fields and they lay out a step-by-step guide for how to create true wealth—enough passive cash flow to cover your expenses.*"

Busting *the* REAL ESTATE INVESTING Lies

Busting *the* REAL ESTATE INVESTING Lies

*Build Wealth the Smart Way:
Through the Most Time-Tested,
Least Volatile Path to Financial Freedom*

KIM BUTLER
with JIMMY VREELAND

prosperityeconomicsmovement

BUSTING THE REAL ESTATE INVESTING LIES
*Building Wealth the Smart Way: Through the Most Time-Tested,
Least Volatile Path to Financial Freedom*

ISBN   978-1-5445-0423-0   *Paperback*
           978-1-5445-0422-3   *Ebook*

Cover design by Michael Nagin
Book & Grahpic design by John van der Woude, JVDW Designs

I want to dedicate this book to my wife, Susie and my kids, Maria, Bubba, Tommy, and Johnny.

—Jimmy Vreeland

I am dedicating this book to my husband, Todd Langford of www. TruthConcepts.com and our children, Jake and Jessica Langford and Robby and Kaylea Butler.

—Kim Butler

CONTENTS

INTRODUCTION

Before the rise of the financial planning industry in the 1970s, the cornerstones of personal finance were "savings accounts, whole life insurance, and the home mortgage." Most people's number one fear was speaking in public, not running out of money.

—Steve Utkus

Do you want to become a millionaire overnight? If so, this book isn't for you! Instead, we are here to teach you how to find true financial freedom through a time-tested, antifragile system. Single-family real estate investing and whole life insurance policies are the means this system uses to achieve financial freedom. The means are important but not as important as the ideas and system that we are going to expose you to in this book.

When most people think about real estate investing, they think flipping houses, and they think high risk, and they probably think about the real estate crash of 2008. What most people know about real estate investing is entirely false. We will debunk the most common lies and show you how to use the time-tested, antifragile strategy of combining real estate and whole life insurance to create wealth. Can financial freedom really be this simple? Does it actually work? Yes! This strategy does require some capital, but the true requirement is a mindset and intellectual curiosity to understand the financial system and how to leverage it.

Let's get started.

THE BIGGEST LIE

Before we begin busting the lies of real estate investing, we'd like to first discuss the biggest lie of all: the myth of the middle class. Here is our working definition of the myth of the middle class: Americans are encouraged to go to school, get a good education and good grades, work hard, pay into a retirement account, buy into mutual funds and qualified plans, and then—after forty years of misery and delaying life—retire and do what we want. Right?

Wrong. We're actually stuck in a rat race. This is not the recipe to get what you want out of life and to live that life to its fullest. This is what we've been told, but it's completely *false*.

Everyone hears this lie, and a lot of people accept it with no questions asked. People are blind to any opportunity that's not hour and dollar related. When you go to work and literally trade hours of your life for a fixed return that you only keep a portion of, that's a limited life. There aren't many ways out of that. It is a tax-disadvantaged environment. We are here to offer alternatives and provide people with options.

THE *APPROVED PLAN* ISN'T WORKING

The idea of retirement is ludicrous, actually. Incomes have stagnated, but expenses have risen. By "saving" money in conventional "retirement" plans, you are speculating on something you have no control over. Typical retirement savings are mathematically impossible. Most Americans live paycheck to paycheck and have no additional funds to invest or save. They are ill-prepared for retirement, and many employers don't even offer retirement plans anymore.

The uncertainty and volatility of the Wall Street casino makes it hard to know which way is up. Your 401(k) investments become 201(k) investments—nearly cut in half based on a stock market crash or extraneous fees. Everything that Wall Street offers is a high-risk, volatile environment. It's an exhausting way to live your life, and this type of retirement plan puts all the risk on the investor for a very small reward. If that's not enough stress, the investor is taxed at ordinary income rates (either up-front or deferred) and pays penalties anytime they want to sell or transfer their money to another investment. If your balance sheet shows $100,000 in a retirement account, cut that value in half. After fees and taxes, that's all you'll be left with. Learn more by watching this video from Truth Concepts: https://youtu.be/GP2d3BhzWBo.

The concept of retirement is flawed and it's hurting people. Those who retire are no longer happy. Human beings need vision and purpose. They need something to do. That basic need doesn't end at the age of sixty-five. Only two-and-a-half generations have had Social Security and retirement even as a concept and available to them, and it is clearly not working. It can actually be detrimental to your health. In the article, "Why retirement can be bad for your health," written by Caroline Parkinson in 2013, the BBC states that retirement "increases the chances of suffering from clinical depression by around 40%, and of having at least one diagnosed physical illness by 60%."[1] Studies also show that working even an extra year has a significant decrease in mortality risk. Healthy retirees show an 11 percent lower mortality risk by staying in their job those extra twelve months.

Humans don't have an inherent need to retire or to stop working, but they do need to sustain their existence. They need to be able to sustain their basic needs of food, water, and shelter. In financial terms, they need to be able to cover their expenses. Retirement messaging is incomplete. People are told that retirement means quitting their jobs, but it should

---

1   Parkinson, Caroline. Second paragraph in "Why retirement can be bad for your health." BBC News. May 16, 2013. Accessed June 7, 2018 https://www.bbc.com/news/health-22553577.

be defined as, "stop trading your precious time for money." In order to achieve this, a person needs enough cash flow to equal their expenses. They need to be able to fund their lives without active income. Conventional retirement plans are supposed to do that, but they are based on deferment plans and are failing miserably.

In essence, the entire concept of retirement is about deferring. We say, "I'll travel when I retire." Or, "I can't take a vacation or do what I want until retirement." We defer our lives and our money, stick our head in the sand, and wake up one day realizing we are at a point where we can't enjoy the money we actually saved.

It's time to make a change.

THE ADVENT OF THE MIDDLE CLASS

We are going to spend the next few paragraphs exposing you to the idea that the middle class is a modern invention.

Before we get started, it's important to acknowledge that we are living in what most would consider the best time to be alive. We are in the full throes of the Information Age, and abundance is created all around us. The Information Age is the period, marked by the onset of the Digital Revolution, that shifted from the Industrial Revolution to an economy based on information technology.

The Sovereign Individual: Mastering the Transition to the Information Age, by James Dale Davidson and Lord William

Rees-Mogg, breaks human history into these frames: the Stone Age, the Agrarian Age, the Industrial Age, and the Information Age.[2] Humanity started hunting and gathering in the Stone Age. Eventually, someone figured out how to make wheat four thousand years ago in Mesopotamia, and the Agricultural Age was born. This time consisted of the royal class, political class, those who owned land, and those who worked the land. Landowners/farmers were essentially small business owners and there wasn't a need for a middle or managing class. The Agricultural Age lasted from approximately 4,000 BC to the 1700s CE. Going back in history, the Stone Age of hunting and gathering led to the Agrarian Age. For nearly two thousand years, people earned their income or sustained their existence through farming. Societies were led by kings, queens, or feudal lords.

The development of capitalism in the 1700s led to the Industrial Age. Before the Industrial Age, almost all labor was done by humans or animals on farms. Now, for the first time in history, humans were able to amass large amounts of capital and create products in mass, generally through the use of machines and factories. Farmers left their farms for factories in the cities. Human society changed and became more urban; the manner in which humans sustained their existence also changed.

---

2   Davidson, James Dale and Lord William Rees-Mogg. "The Fourth Stage of Human Society. In The Sovereign Individual: Mastering the Transition to the Information Age, 1st Touchstone Edition, p. 15. New York: Touchstone, 1999.

Instead of working as small independent farmers, humans now worked as cogs in a large labor and capital intensive machine. Large industry generated the need for a "managing" class to manage these workers. A variety of societal changes took place during the Industrial Age that are well outside the scope of this book, but it's important to note that the concept of the middle class is distinctly tied to this time period. The economy and government became industrialized as well. The education system changed to create managers to manage the industrial system. Unfortunately, education has not updated itself in order to produce sovereign individuals capable of creating and adapting to change inside the Information Age.

The concept of retirement was also introduced during the Industrial Age. During the Stone Age, you were lucky to live past the age of thirty, and if you did, you weren't granted a pass by the rest of the tribe to sit on your rear-end while they hunted and gathered for you. During the Agricultural Age, the farmer didn't reach the age of fifty and then get to sit in his rocking chair on the porch while everyone farmed his land. The idea of retirement is a monster created during the Industrial Age by bureaucrats. They needed citizens with no assets or land to go to state schools, become a manager, worker, or soldier, and then work until they were no longer needed or productive. At that point, the bureaucrat needed the ability to push the older worker somewhere to make sure there was a job for a younger worker. Young, unemployed workers create civil unrest; older ones do not.

The bureaucrats also needed to garner votes from the older population and the easiest way to do so was to promise the golden ticket of "Retirement." The American bureaucrats created "Social Security." As most of us know, Social Security was started at a time when the average life expectancy was much shorter and also assumes population growth would continue at the same pace. Neither of these things turned out to be true and the promises the government made can no longer be met.

Around 1990, we moved into the Information Age. The factory was now less valuable than the spread of information. Information does not require much capital or labor to create value. Unfortunately, the middle class began to lose value, too. With every day that passes, technology or cheaper labor is available to take over middle-class jobs and positions.

What we currently call the middle class is a historical anomaly. It's been around for maybe eighty years. It was clearly built for the Industrial Age, not the Information Age. This strategy that we are going to expose to you is going to seem new and unconventional, but really it's more of a throwback. It's been time tested and you'll see that there are a lot of similarities between the Agrarian Age and the new Information Age, because large companies and large bureaucracies are no longer essential; they most likely will still exist but they will not be necessary for the system to work. This strategy is not dependent on large state, large government, bureaucratic, or corporate apparatus.

Age	Man	Occupation
Agrarian	Mother and father with family all day on the farm.	Farmer, small business owner, entrepreneur.
Industrial	Cog in a machine, away from family, or a manager/ bureaucrat managing the cogs in the machine.	Factory worker, manager, soldier, corporate employee, government worker.
Information	Working from home, modern day hunter/ gatherer is on the laptop. Less need for industrialized-style work.	Small business entrepreneurs, less need for big organizations. Radical decentralization.

We are setting this frame to show you that the Industrial Age was not a phenomenon that lasted long, and several institutions created during this time will change, adapt, or go extinct. The investment strategy we are about to show you has stood the test of time.

STANDING THE TEST OF TIME

This better way isn't a new way, it's actually one that has stood the test of time. Over the past 200 years, the one consistent performer in building wealth has been real estate coupled with whole life insurance. (Please note, this does not work with term insurance, which only provides coverage for a specific time period and does not accumulate cash value or allow you to borrow money against it.)

Historically, the greatest producer of wealth has been real estate, but real estate investing is a poor word choice because it can mean a variety of things; for example, a company owning a skyscraper invests in real estate, but so does an individual who owns one rental property.

Wealth was built inside this country by homesteading and developing property. A piece of property was either homesteaded or purchased, that land was then made productive through farming the soil, extracting resources, or adding a building. This strategy created a great amount of wealth over the past 250 years. What most people don't understand is that coupled along with these real estate investments were whole life insurance policies. A pioneer or large landowner didn't add value into the land or building, make money, build wealth, and then send their profits off to Manhattan. The banking system wasn't stable enough (Google wildcat banking). In fact, for the last 200 years, nearly every twenty years there has been some type of recession or banking crisis. In order to generate money, you had to collect outside of the system. So they took profits and put them inside a whole life insurance policy.

This strategy worked just fine until the 1950s and 1960s, when a bunch of number crunchers, eggheads, and bureaucrats got together—without practitioners (people doing the day-to-day work)—in a room to start planning. To nobody's surprise, bad things happened. The College of Financial Planning in Denver created what we know today as a financial plan by using averages and assumptions to calculate projections for someone's financial life.

Unfortunately, financial plans aren't exactly realistic. Economics isn't physics and can't be analyzed in a controlled environment that refuses to take into consideration volatility, human emotions, and technological change. One of our favorite quotes is from Yogi Berra, "In theory, there is no difference between practice and theory. In practice, there is."

Forgoing reality, everybody jumped on board to the concept of financial planning because it was able to be sold as a product to the masses. It didn't matter if it worked or not. We maxed out our 401(k) contributions every year, bought term insurance, and prepaid our mortgages. Any remaining money we shoved into the stock market and mutual funds.

Why? Advisors told us to, and they also told us Wall Street could get us rich fast. It is human nature to want something for nothing. Humans want to put a little money in and get a lot out. Humans are also impatient and don't want to dig deep to find strategic solutions, so they delegate their finances to a planner.

Most people also don't understand inflation. Taking the dollar off the gold standard was a subsidy to Wall Street. The government could print money at will, so the Cantillon effect took place. All commodities and stocks rose in value, but they weren't getting more buying power. It created a rush because people saw that the security was higher. The nominal value of the stock price went up, giving the appearance that the returns were higher than they actually were. If you broke it down and removed the inflation, the rise wasn't nearly as substantial. Financial planners took advantage of this, saying, "Securities will go up 8 percent. Invest all your money there!" At one point, returns were an easy 20 percent. Everyone thought this would continue forever.

LOOKING AT THE DOW OVER 100 YEARS

In the year 1900, the Dow Jones Industrial Average was 65.29. One hundred years later, it was 11,600. Using a Rate Calculator, we can see that 65 growing to 11,600 over 100 years results in an Annual Interest Rate of 5.32%. So the Dow has averaged 5.32% over those 100 years.

Rate Calculator			_ □ X
Present Value: 65.00	Title	Clear	N E W
Annual Payment: 0.00	• Beg	○ End	
Future Value: 11,600	A M Q S		T O P
Years: 100.00	• ○ ○ ○		
Annual Int. Rate: 5.32%			

How can we use that to project over the next 100 years? We use a Future Value Calculator and input 11,600 as the Present Value and 5.32% for the Annual Interest Rate. From there, we see that the Dow will have to be at 2,067,964 in the year 2100 to have averaged a 5.32% annual interest rate during the next 100 years.

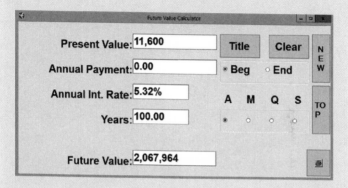

Unfortunately, an inflationary environment encourages speculation. Money sitting in a box under your bed actually loses value and power. People recognize this over time and realize they can't just save; they have to invest. Unfortunately, people are encouraged to speculate on Wall Street. We will explain this later in the book, but conventional financial planning is speculating, *not* investing.

Robert Kiyosaki says that savers are losers.[3] This sound bite gets caught in a loop, but the deeper explanation doesn't get shared. This is not sound-bite material. A *saver* can be a noun or a verb. When a saver is a noun, Kiyosaki is correct. If you are a

---

3   Kiyosaki, Robert. "Why Savers are Losers." www.richdad.com. October 17, 2005. Accessed June 7, 2018 http://www.richdad.com/Resources/Articles/why-savers-are-losers.aspx.

saver and your money sits in a savings account, inflation and taxes will kill you. The value of money that sits erodes over time and you lose purchasing power. But if you use the word *saver* as a verb meaning *stores liquidity*, that's what everyone should do. You then use that liquidity for the purpose of an opportunity fund, which we will discuss later on. The verb saver is a *winner*, not a loser.

In our system, where should someone store their liquidity? In a bank, right? Nope; we are going to show you how to use a time-tested but unconventional strategy of using whole life policies as a bank. The first step in our system is save/store liquidity. You can never save yourself to financial independence, but it is a first step. Storing liquidity inside a whole life policy and using the liquidity to begin to invest in real estate is a consistent path to financial freedom. This strategy is also distinctly American, and it is one of the privileges of living in this country. The bedrock of the US financial and legal system is contract law—both real estate investing and life insurance rely and only exist because of American contract law—we will explain more in the next section.

THE AMERICAN BENEFITS

We often get objections from people asking why they should invest in real estate or put money in a whole life insurance policy. Our response is, "What does the bank and whole life insurance company invest in?" After a pause, they usually act chagrined and say, "Oh. Real estate."

Exactly. Real estate. So why not cut out the middleman and do it yourself?

Consider this for a moment: a bank won't lend you money to purchase stocks or mutual funds, but they will loan you money to purchase real estate. They will also loan you money against your whole life insurance, which is a clue to why these two assets work so well together. Banks will not lend money against a qualified plan, because they know they are inherently too risky and if there is a crash, the bank loses all of its collateral. Banks understand and will lend against the cash value of life insurance and a piece of property because both have acceptable collateral. If the owner of a piece of property defaults, the bank can take an asset back (the house). If the owner of a life insurance policy defaults, the bank can take the actual cash of the life insurance policy as collateral.

Americans, through 200 years of struggle, have created the best contract and title law in economic history. People talk about American exceptionalism, but rarely do they consider the underlying reason or foundation as to why Americans have been able to create so much wealth, and why entrepreneurship is so strong in this country. We have the strongest contract and title law in the world. You can buy a piece of land or property, extract value out of that piece of land, and leverage it for liquidity—all because you can show proper title to what you own. You can divide your property, sell shares of it, or even borrow against it. It is more than just brick and mortar; it is now an asset.

In most third-world countries, people do not own and cannot show clear title to even own the land that they live on and the house that they live in. Their savings are tied up into the walls of the house, and they can't access the money. In contrast, we can take advantage of our property law, and it's the basis for how we are so economically strong. For further in-depth discussion of this concept, check out Hernando De Soto's excellent book, *The Mystery of Capital: Why Capitalism Triumphs in the West and Fails Everywhere Else.*

Whole life insurance also exists and works because of contract law. It fills an essential need in the market and is an effective way to replace the income of the breadwinners in the family, if necessary. Entrepreneurs created this system, basing it on a contract between the company and the policyholder. On the flip side, bureaucrats and politicians created retirement plans based off regulation and legislation to fulfill the political need to replace the pension system.

It is very easy to change regulation and legislation based on the political environment; Congress could—and we think will—alter the current qualified retirement plan legislation to meet their immediate political needs. Congress cannot change whole life insurance contracts without rewriting contract law, and that would affect real estate, banking, and other financial institutions, so it's extremely unlikely to happen.

Furthermore, the whole life insurance contract is unilateral. The company is obligated to you, but you are not obligated to it. We want to be obligated because being obligated to it is to be obligated to ourselves. The traditional whole life insurance contract or policy is held inside a mutual company owned by the policyholders. There are no shares, it's not public, and you can't buy a piece of it unless you buy a policy. That mutual structure gives contract law even more emphasis, because the people controlling the company are the owners of the policy that also own the company.

Contract law also allows for generational wealth. Property is very easy to pass on—whether to your children, a family member, or even a charity. You can sell shares of the property or trade it, turning it into capital which moves faster and is scalable.

As Americans, we literally have the golden ticket in our hands with our access to real estate and whole life insurance.

THE STRATEGY

Real estate is not liquid, so you can't invest solely in real estate. Whole life insurance doesn't create income streams the way real estate does, so you can't only purchase whole life insurance. Together, they are the perfect combination of liquidity and cash flow. On paper, it may not look sexy, but you'll find comfort in the knowledge that you're leveraging tax benefits, you're investing instead of speculating, and you're operating in a very nonvolatile environment. This is an antifragile strategy that leverages the current financial system to mitigate the downside and avoid the risk of ruin that exists on Wall Street.

The best investors on the planet know the secret to growing money is not making huge gains—it's making sure to never take a loss. Losing money can set you back years.

This strategy has been used for the last few hundred years. According to *Pirates of Manhattan* by Barry Dyke, every large bank uses whole life insurance as their primary vehicle to store liquidity.[4] If most large banks are using it, why aren't they passing this idea down to people on Main Street? Because they want you to buy their products, and then they want to put their profits from you buying their products into a system that actually works. Think about it: banks take your deposits, loan them to real estate investors, and earn the high rates of return themselves. They arbitrage your money for their own benefit. This is why we say to cut out the middleman and do it yourself—keeping all the upside to yourself. All that's required is a little bit of know-how, which you will have by the time you finish reading this book.

It's time to keep your money to yourself and choose your own investments wisely.

LIQUIDITY IN TIMES OF VOLATILITY

The antifragile investor loves randomness and uncertainty. By not following the crowd, you can use randomness and uncertainty to your advantage. It all goes back to the old saying, "Buy

---

4   Dyke, Barry. *Pirates of Manhattan*. Hampton, NH: Self-Published, Castle Asset Management, LLC, 2008.

	Real Estate	Insurance Policy	Real Estate and an Insurance Policy
Cash Flow	Cash flow in the form of monthly rent—best thing about real estate.	Cash flow in the form of annual dividends.	Same dollars are working for you in two places at once. Receive cash flow from both simultaneously.
Appreciation	Most likely will occur but possible market crashes cause short-term losses.	Guaranteed return based on a dollar figure—principal never at risk.	Same dollars can appreciate in two places simultaneously.
Tax Advantages	Passive income taxed lower; long-term capital gains lower; able to write off depreciation.	Tax-deferred compounding dividends. Death benefit is passed to heirs tax free.	Same dollars can receive tax benefits of both asset classes simultaneously.
Equity	Principal pay down on amortization schedule and possible appreciation over time builds equity.	Insurance policy is an asset on your balance sheet. Death benefit increases over time.	Both assets will improve any investor's balance sheet. Same dollars build equity in both simultaneously.
Leverage	Smaller down payment controls larger asset and increases ROI.	Smaller annual premium controls larger asset. Can use cash value as collateral.	Same dollars can serve as premium and down payment on house and can control both assets at the same time.
Inflation Hedge	Use bank money to purchase and pay back long-term loans with inflated dollars. Rents/property values increase with inflation.	Use insurance company money to acquire assets and pay back loan with inflated dollars. Dividend increases if inflation increases.	Use loans from banks and insurance companies and pay back loans with inflated dollars.

when there's blood in the streets." The liquidity created inside the whole life insurance policy allows an investor to invest during a crash. The people most hurt during the late 2008 crash were those in a liquidity crunch, because they couldn't invest in anything that would provide them with cash flow. However, if you sat on a bunch of cash, it was go-time. You bought everything you could get your hands on, at the bottom, and were able to hold onto them for the long haul, because the properties supported themselves with cash flow. You could sell later, when the market returned, for huge upside.

Antifragility is beyond resilience or robustness. The resilient resist shock and stay the same; the antifragile are at their best in times of high volatility.

COMING TO THE REALIZATION

We are the first to admit we didn't always invest this way. It took some eye-opening moments for us to buy into the whole life insurance and real estate strategy and for us to come together to write this book. Here's a quick peek into our pasts and how we came to discover this life-changing strategy.

Jimmy

I left the military with a high suspicion of bureaucrats, and my first day as a civilian was the day investment banking giant Bear Stearns collapsed. I felt like the bureaucrats and the government had not only just screwed up the war I was fighting in, but now they were in charge of investment banking and messing that up, too. I was a high-paid w-2 and killing it, but I was stuck giving half of it to the government and the rest was spent on bills for my family. I was staring down the barrel of a gun where I would be forced to do the exact same work, living under the exact same pressures, for the next thirty years. Human beings act to alleviate anxieties and to expand. They act in order to continue to make their short time on earth constantly better. Working for money, giving that money to the government in taxes, and then giving up even more to financial institutions that you do not control—and repeating this pattern for forty years—does not reduce anxiety or lead to expansion. It is asinine. Every January 1, I'd get a new quota in the same life-sucking game. I knew I had to find something different.

I love this country and I was willing to fight for it. When I say fight for it I mean that sincerely. I was not a staff officer who sat behind a desk; I was on the front lines. I was willing to get shot at, blown up, jump out of planes, walk for miles, and spend time in the worst parts of the world—all for my country. I still am. But when I got home and started earning money, I was not willing to give up 40-50 percent of the fruits of my labor. That was the dividing line for me. I realized that my government is not my country and the people I loved. To be a patriot does not mean to support the political party that is in power at the time; to be a patriot means to support and defend the liberties of your fellow citizens.

Once I discovered *Rich Dad Poor Dad*, real estate investing, and entrepreneurship, I saw a new way to fight for freedom. I was heavily influenced by Tom Wheelwright, who shows that there is a patriotic way to legally pay zero taxes. It may be an even more effective way to fight. If I lived in the Middle Ages or during the time of the Revolutionary War, I would take up arms to fight for freedom. We now live in a time of abundance. Luckily, I don't have to fight with guns, but there is still a fight to be had with assets and money. I wanted to write this book in order to take a stand and show people that there is a simple, but not easy, strategy from which they can leverage the current system and fight for their own economic freedom.

The myth of the middle class is a load of s*** and there is no way that the wealthiest and most productive people in all of human history should spend their lives shackled to jobs that they hate and rob their families of their time, only to give 40 percent of the money to the government and another 10 percent of their money to the financial planning industry that puts their money at a high level of risk for a minimal return. Only a sucker would take all of the risk in any investment and that is what you are doing in a qualified retirement plan. Tax-deferred is not tax-free, and only a sucker would pay ordinary income rates on investments.

Kim

I graduated from college and worked in a bank where I received typical financial planning training. During my time at the bank, I had many entrepreneurial clients and real estate clients. The typical financial plan strategy was a punch in the stomach when I realized it didn't work, and it was all a lie. I knew it could be mathematically accurate, but realistically it was completely debunked because math has nothing to do with people's lives. I had learned how the entrepreneurs at the bank built, stored, and protected their wealth. That was an important realization, because I had seen real estate investors who had no cash and got stuck, and entrepreneurs who had also been educated on whole life insurance and the use of policies as liquidity. I put two and two together and continued to progress from there.

Fast forward to today and our family now uses whole life insurance as our emergency opportunity fund and a savings account with a "bill." What I mean by this is that the premium notice shows up every month and has forced us to save in a way we never would have. We have cash value that has supported our lives and emergency funds, to be used when we needed additional money to make payroll or for opportunities to improve the home. We used the whole life insurance cash value as needed and then always paid it back. That's very important.

We also borrowed against the cash value for investments, like real estate, that created cash flow that helped us pay the whole life insurance back. We invested on our own and with Jimmy. We realized doing it on our own was not our area of Unique Ability® and our dollars were better spent with their model.

Together

Like attracts like, and the two of us eventually found our way to each other; real estate and whole life insurance combined. This changed the paradigm completely. There is this constant velocity of movement of money through whole life insurance and into real estate, which is then enabling the cash flow to come back and help pay off the whole life insurance loan. We both implement this strategy now.

One family's goal may be just to get enough real estate to pay expenses. Another family's goal may be to pay back the cash value of the whole life insurance so they can buy more real estate, create more money, and focus on the next thing they want to do. Perhaps they want to build a business, create a nonprofit, or get involved in charity. We want to help those people have better practices. Instead of just having whole life insurance or real estate, they can have whole life insurance and real estate, and it enables their financial picture to be so much stronger.

We want to help and we decided to write this book to educate and empower others to create their own wealth. We want to help you before it's too late, before you are misled to go down the mass-marketed path, and before you believe the lies being fed to you.

WHAT ARE THE LIES?

Most of what you believe regarding real estate investing is wrong:

- **It takes too much money.** No. You don't have to buy the houses. Leverage the banking system and put down the minimal down payment. Leverage, used correctly, is one of the most powerful tools for any investor.

- **It takes too much time.** No. You will not be spending time looking at houses, evaluating properties, putting together estimates on repairs, managing contractors, placing tenants, or managing tenants.

- **It's too complicated.** No. We have simple metrics to show you that it's about cash flow, not appreciation. When you remove a lot of irrelevant information from the equation, it can be very quick and easy to identify good investments.

- **It's too risky.** No. We will remove the intimidation factor out of trying to identify a good real estate investment. We will systematically show you that it is not as risky as what you're currently doing on Wall Street. When you invest for cash flow, it removes most of the outside factors, like market volatility.

- **It's about flipping.** No. The HGTV lineup on flipping houses is a lie. We'll teach you why it's important to hold onto and rent out your properties for the long term.

Whole life insurance also has lies that need to be busted:

- **It's an investment.** No. It's actually a place to store cash. And you don't have to borrow against the insurance for it to be effective.

- **It's multi-level marketing.** No. Whole life insurance companies were typically created by a church or community that came together to put money in a pot if a family had a death, so it didn't destroy the family. The idea of mutual ownership was built on that concept. Everyone contributes and everyone benefits. Private individuals and organizations saw this need and fulfilled it with companies like GoFundMe—where two-thirds of the campaigns are due to a death in the family where the breadwinner was not insured.

- **It's too expensive.** No. Term insurance is certainly cheaper than whole life insurance, but the benefits are drastically different.

- **It's federally regulated.** No. It's state regulated and doesn't have a lot of the issues that come with the banks and large corporate investments that require federal regulation.

WHAT CAN YOU EXPECT?

The following eight chapters will provide you with the path to financial freedom through real estate investing and cash value whole life insurance. This is not about making millionaires overnight. It's about building wealth and freeing up time by creating passive income that goes straight to your mailbox.

This isn't theory. The results are proven, and this is how we all make money. If you read the rest of this book and follow our strategies—assuming you have capital built up—we can get you antifragile cash flow in ninety days. If you need to build a base of capital, it might take a little longer.

Imagine this scenario: you have a portfolio of cash-flowing properties. You may still have a career you love, but now you have the option to take time off, try a different career field, study, or travel. Most people won't retire, sit back, and relax. They want to live their life, and it's important to have as much autonomy as possible. This strategy provides options and offers peace of mind. You're not checking your portfolio balance every day or watching the stock market ticker and living on every up and down mark. You're not worried in times of crisis.

Instead, you can sleep at night. You've put yourself in a position where you're almost untouchable when it comes to financial risks. Imagine how a life like that would feel.

If this life is something you want, read on.

Chapter 1
SET YOUR STRIKE NUMBER

We are on strike, we, the men of the mind.

We are on strike against self-immolation. We are on strike against the creed of unearned rewards and unrewarded duties. We are on strike against the dogma that the pursuit of one's happiness is evil. We are on strike against the doctrine that life is guilt.

—Ayn Rand, *Atlas Shrugged*

The first step in finding financial freedom is for you to determine your end goal. We call this a *strike number*, and it refers to the cash flow you need to cover your monthly expenses. From there, we will show you how to calculate the number of houses/properties you need to invest in to reach your goal.

WHAT IS A STRIKE NUMBER?

Jimmy Gets His Time Back

The term *strike number* refers to the income needed for you to go on strike from your job (should you choose) and to go on strike from 50 percent of your income being taken away from you. I came up with the concept when I realized so much of my income was being taxed by the government and, after reading *Atlas Shrugged*, I wanted to go on strike. I no longer wanted to work in a hamster-wheel job, so I used the idea of a strike number from *Rich Dad Poor Dad*, but I put a twist on it. My version of the strike number is defined as the cash flow required to equal my expenses. When I hit that number, I wouldn't need to work for anyone else anymore.

I worked in medical sales prior to real estate investing, but as I began to accumulate properties, I realized I didn't have to keep starting over every year with my medical sales quota requirements. I worked my way up to earning one thousand dollars a month on the five properties I owned. I continued to invest and obtained more properties to make two thousand dollars a month. Eventually, the cash flow became ten thousand dollars a month.

This was my strike number.

I knew I could quit and get my time back, because it didn't matter if I worked or not. I had now invested in approximately fifty homes with income of $200 each a month, which is a conservative estimate and reproducible for investors.

The beauty of cash flow was the ability to continue working while building the initial investments. The only work was to open my mailbox and pull out the $200 check each month. That money felt better than the $20,000 a month I was bringing home from my sales position!

THE SIGNIFICANCE OF THE STRIKE NUMBER

When you set your brain on a number, it focuses on a concrete dollar amount and the *why* of what you're doing. If you don't have that specific number, your brain wanders aimlessly without focus. There's no accountability or measuring stick. You don't know if you've made it. Once you have the goal written down, your subconscious mind will automatically go to work for you, and as long as you don't lose sight of it, you'll soon achieve it.

The strike number helps narrow down options, and you'll find you won't go after anything—not with your money or your time—that doesn't contribute toward hitting that amount. The beauty of the strike number is the simplicity surrounding the focus. It's a monthly amount. You don't have to start Facebook or Google or some massive technology company. You don't need to win the lottery. This isn't about luck; it's about keeping it simple and working smarter.

Unfortunately, when people invest using the typical financial planning methodology, they don't know how much they should be saving. Their goal is only to shove money into their

IRA or 401(k) and hope there's enough money on the flip side when it comes time to retire.

A strike number is strategic, systematic, and attainable. This is drastically different from how people typically view real estate investing. They think they need to have a large down payment to get a nice piece of property that's going to appreciate and they can sell for a huge profit in a few years. It's not about the home runs. It's about easy, repeatable base hits that provide cash flow that adds up over time. If you're scared of dealing with tenants, don't worry. We've got the solution for you later in the book.

CASH FLOW VS. NET WORTH

The typical financial planning industry centers around net worth, but net worth does not put food on the table. It doesn't create experiences or pay for vacations. Net worth is a measuring stick that is, frankly, irrelevant. Many people think being a millionaire is the goal, when in reality you can be a millionaire on paper when it comes to net worth, but actually be broke when it comes to having money to pay your bills. Net worth can fluctuate wildly based on market volatility. A paradigm shift is required, and you need to focus on cash flow as opposed to net worth.

Most people don't know how to convert net worth into income. The good news is you're different and reading this book will teach you how.

A retiree may have $400,000 in their 401(k) rollover but have absolutely no idea what the next steps are to create an income—especially consistent monthly income that doesn't rise and fall with the stock market. It requires starting small and with a strategy.

THE LIE

The lie of this chapter is that real estate investing is about speculating, buying for appreciation and accumulating net worth.

Wrong.

When most people buy for appreciation, they are putting their financial life into the hands of outside forces. Greater macroeconomic forces come into play: interest rates, how loose/tight bank lending is at any given time, how much money the federal reserve decides to print, and the general feeling people have towards the real estate market at the time. You are also subject to a wide variety of more local geographic forces: how many people are moving in and out of the area, job growth or lack thereof, and the amount of new construction being built every year. You have no control over any of these things. You can do your best to anticipate market cycles, but nobody has a crystal ball, and dealing with the ups and downs isn't worth the hassle quite frankly. Hoping and praying the market goes up is no way to build a solid financial picture.

WHAT IS CASH FLOW?

Cash flow is the amount of money a property produces after paying its expenses every month. With most properties, you generate income from what the tenant pays you in rent every month and subtract the expenses. The typical expenses on a single-family home are principal and interest payments, prorated taxes and insurance, management fees, along with holding some money in reserves for vacancy, repairs, and maintenance.

Cash Flow = Income - Expenses

To eliminate as much risk and outside forces as possible from your investing game plan, you need to focus on building a portfolio of cash-flowing assets. Values of property can swing wildly, but rents do not fluctuate as much on a percentage basis in a down market. If your properties are kicking off cash flow every month, you don't necessarily care what the overall market is doing. On paper, the property you own could be worth 30 percent less, but it still makes you money every month. This money pays the bills and puts food on the table.

This strategy is not about making lots of money through appreciation. Our method of investing is about getting your time back and thus your mind back. You obtain cash flow, you use that money to buy more properties, which kick off more income, and the cycle repeats. The goal is to create a life of freedom today.

In *The 4-Hour Work Week*, Tim Ferris encourages readers to consider whether retirement makes sense and whether they can really enjoy life when they're at an age when they physically can't do as many things.[5] We encourage you to rethink the concept of retirement and create options for the present moment instead of putting them off for several decades. You never know what will happen in life. Don't push goals and opportunities into some obscure future date; build a solid plan that sets you up for success today, and tomorrow will take care of itself as a by-product.

STRIKE NUMBER CALCULATOR

Current monthly expenses: _____

Average cash flow per house
($250 is a good target): _____

Monthly expenses/Average cash flow = _____ houses

GET YOUR TIME BACK

Instead of dying sick, let's focus on dying healthy. Let's get your time back. Let's get you peace of mind with financial freedom. You will no longer have to work a fifty-hour workweek with

---

5   Ferriss, Timothy. *The 4-Hour Workweek: Escape 9-5, Live Anywhere, and Join the New Rich*, pp. all. New York: Crown Publishers, 2009.

two weeks of vacation each year. Instead, you can die healthy without the typical stresses of the corporate work world.

Time is man's scarcest and most valuable resource. When your time is your own, you can be a better partner and parent. You can make better business decisions. You can study and focus on your Unique Abilities®. You can make better decisions from a place of abundance versus a place of lack and scarcity.

Even more than that, when you arrive home, you're not walking in the door feeling exhausted and whipped. You don't need to offload the stress of a demanding job. You're excited and rejuvenated, and your relationships are the better for it.

TAKING THE DETOUR

This detour from typical financial planning will happen at some point in your life. Whether you decide to do it now voluntarily or wait until the reality of another market crash turns your 401(k) into a 201(k)—thus waking you up. It's your call.

At some point, you have to be diligent and proactive about taking a portion of income—whether it's earned income from your day job or passive real estate income—and start the very long term, very slow process of building a whole life insurance policy to be used as your emergency/opportunity fund for the rest of your life.

You have your strike number and a strategy to achieve financial freedom through buying cash-flowing real estate. Now it's time to create a foundation. Whole life insurance helps you get there more efficiently, on more solid ground, and with a better foundation. And with that solid base, you'll build and protect your wealth. You will create an emergency/opportunity fund that will continue to grow as you build a larger wealth environment.

Chapter 2
ESTABLISH YOUR EMERGENCY/ OPPORTUNITY FUND

If you have not acquired more than a bare existence in the years since we were youths, it is because you either have failed to learn the laws that govern the building of wealth, or else you do not observe them. A part of all you earn is yours to keep. It should be not less than a tenth no matter how little you earn. It can be as much more as you can afford. Pay yourself first.

—George Samuel Clason, *The Richest Man in Babylon*[6]

Most people are familiar with the concept of an emergency fund, a safety net for when the unexpected happens, like a sudden job loss, a broken transmission, or medical

6 Clason, George Samuel. "The Richest Man in Babylon Tells His System," In *The Richest Man in Babylon*, pp. 13, 16. La Vergne, TN: BN Publishing, 2008.

expenses. Savings save families. Emergencies aren't fun to think about or save for, though, and as a result, too many people never establish a sufficient safety net. Instead, you should focus on building an emergency/opportunity fund. Saving for opportunities is much more exciting than saving for emergencies.

Each individual and family will have a different target baseline for their emergency fund—the amount needed to sleep well at night without constant money worries about handling the basic necessities in case of an emergency. For some people, it may be $1,000; for others, it may be $10,000 or even $1,000,000. A common guideline is to have enough saved that you could pay three months' worth of bills. This is a good starting place, and as time grows, this amount can grow too.

Once you hit your emergency baseline, you can keep saving more and more, earmarking all of those additional funds for opportunities. As you get older, your emergency/opportunity fund will get bigger, and more opportunities will be available to you. In order to take full advantage of your emergency/opportunity fund, you want these assets to be liquid, and you do that through a whole life insurance policy.

UNLOCKING YOUR MONEY

Kim's Client Who Found His Hands Tied

I had a client in Pennsylvania who was doing everything according to the typical financial planning model. He prepaid his mortgage, maxed out his contributions to his qualified retirement plan (putting in even more than his employer's match), and funded his kids' 529 plans. He had also bought only term life insurance. He thought he was doing everything right. He was following all the typical advice, after all.

His wife, a hairdresser at a high-end salon, decided she wanted to establish some savings of her own. Their financial advisor recommended an SEP, a kind of qualified retirement plan. They didn't feel good about having their money locked up until age fifty-nine and a half, though. They were both young, and they were good savers, with good discipline. As they looked for other options, they came across one of my first books, *Busting Financial Planning Lies*, and it rocked their world, as my recommendations went against everything they'd been told to do. They didn't think I could possibly be right about everything, but they were curious and open-minded enough to seek me out for further advice. That open-mindedness was critical. I would be undoing nearly everything they had been doing, and I would not have been able to help them if they weren't open to a new approach.

They were right to be concerned and seek other options because they had one gigantic issue: they lacked liquidity. All their money was locked up. The qualified retirement plan, the mortgage equity, the 529s—they had money saved but couldn't access any of it. They did have an emergency fund, but it was the typical $10,000 sitting in a bank somewhere doing nothing. That money could help them out in a worst-case scenario, but it wasn't enough to allow them to pursue opportunities.

This client discovered that fact the hard way. An amazing opportunity presented itself to him: he had the chance to invest in the company he worked for and become an owner instead of an employee. While that opportunity was exciting, it also meant a big transition. He would stop earning a guaranteed salary and would begin to be paid as an owner, with earnings dependent on the business's success or failure. He also required money to make changes to the business. In order to take advantage of this opportunity, he needed cash, but it was all locked up. He had followed the typical path and didn't have the flexibility to pursue an opportunity when it came knocking.

This couple had been doing everything wrong and suffered as a result. When I came in, I encouraged several changes. I had the husband drop his qualified retirement plan contributions to the employer match level instead of maxing them out. I had them drop their 529 contributions entirely and stop prepaying their fifteen-year mortgage (they still had to make monthly payments for the mortgage, but they were no longer prepaying).

I left their term life insurance in place, as term insurance is fine as long as it's not used for long-term purposes. A term life insurance policy is temporary; it's for a certain period, or term, of time—one year, five years, ten years, or so on. It can give people peace of mind that they are protected for that period of time, but luckily, most people do not die in that term of time. With most insurance, like car insurance or health insurance, there's no guaranteed event requiring a payout—no guaranteed car accident, no guaranteed illness—but death is a guaranteed event. It's important to tie your life insurance to that guaranteed event, and that's what whole life insurance does. Whole life insurance comes with three guarantees: the policy is guaranteed to pay out eventually, the policy's premium isn't going to change, and the policy has a guaranteed cash value, which is a dollar figure, not an interest rate. Those guarantees do come with a higher cost, but it's worth it. Whole life insurance has created a very boring—yet very effective—structural foundation that allows people to store wealth and to build wealth while retaining liquidity.

It's important to not confuse whole life insurance with universal life insurance. Beginning around the mid-twentieth century, universal life insurance began to be sold as if it had all the guarantees of whole life insurance, but in reality, it was term insurance with a savings account, like a money market account that is subject to interest rate fluctuations. These universal life insurance policies do not have a guaranteed premium, guaranteed cash value, or guaranteed death benefit, which is constantly increasing like whole life does.

So while I left my clients' term life insurance in place, I made sure they added whole life insurance as well. I had them put all the money they were now saving each month toward a monthly contribution to a whole life insurance policy with high cash value. With that, they began to build an opportunity fund on top of their emergency fund.

Within a few years, my clients were in a position to refinance their home to a thirty-year mortgage and drop their monthly payments. They were then able to establish a second whole life insurance policy with the savings.

Within a few more years, thanks to his new opportunity fund, my client was able to start the ownership transition process at his place of work. A few more years passed, and he was able to invest in real estate and buy a commercial building. As he and his wife made more money, they continued to open whole life insurance policies. They could then borrow against the whole life insurance cash value for more real estate investing. Financially, they're in a much stronger position today, and it all began with an emergency/opportunity fund.

THE IMPORTANCE OF LIQUIDITY

To invest in real estate the right way, you need to have a source of liquidity and to make your first real estate deal, you'll need a lump sum. However, contrary to common perception, you actually don't need a lot of capital to invest in real estate. At a minimum, you need only $15,000. That's the absolute bare minimum to have as a down payment on cash-flowing property in the Midwest United States, including closing costs. We really recommend that you have $25,000, and we prefer to work with clients who have closer to $50,000.

Why do we recommend having more? Well, if everything goes perfectly, $15,000 would be fine, but things rarely go perfectly in life. You need to have an extra $10,000 cushion, on top of your personal emergency fund, for when problems inevitably crop up. Otherwise, if you put all your money into deals, when one little thing goes wrong—say a furnace goes out on one of your properties—you won't have any liquid capital available to fix it. Or if a property goes vacant, you might need to cover two months of expenses. There are ups and downs that will occasionally happen, and you don't ever want to find yourself suddenly in the position of being the motivated seller, needing to liquidate fast. That is the quickest way to have your real estate dreams go up in smoke. Be wary of anyone who encourages you to tie up all your capital. You should never put your last dime into real estate. It's much better to wait until you have an adequate cushion. Remember, a key component of this strategy is removing the stress of the ups and downs of market cycles. If you tie up all your liquid savings, you'll be right back into the stress trap.

HOW TO GET TO YOUR THRESHOLD

The way you get to this $25,000 threshold is through whole life insurance. You could save this amount at a credit union or bank, but then your money is just sitting in an account not doing anything. You actually lose money because of inflation, as we discussed earlier. Saving through a whole life insurance policy takes a little bit longer, but it's more efficient and effective because those savings dollars are active, working for you in a multitude of ways and allowing you to get into real estate from a much stronger position. Many people choose to make use of a line of credit (LOC) or a home equity line of credit (HELOC), but the issue is that a LOC or HELOC is not your money, and you do not control it. If there's an economic downturn or a liquidity crunch, you're not getting that money back. People often don't understand how quickly banks will cut your line of credit in times of economic turmoil.

If you already have $25,000 saved up, great! But for most people, hitting this threshold can be a challenge, especially for those new to saving. Part of the beauty of using whole life insurance is that the funds are liquid but not easily accessible. This makes saving to the threshold amount easier. If you put a set amount into a checking or savings account each month, it's easy to pull that money right back out. You simply swipe your debit card, and the money is spent. But with whole life insurance, you pay the monthly bill, and if you want to use the money or borrow against it, you have to request it. You can still get it quickly, perhaps within twenty-four to seventy-two hours, depending on the company. But, this one little step forces you to stop and think, *What am I using this money for? Am I using it for the right reasons?* That moment of conscious awareness ensures you are living by the principle of paying yourself first, one of the lessons from the great book, *The Richest Man in Babylon*, written by George Samuel Clason.

He writes, "If you have not acquired more than a bare existence in the years since we were youths, it is because you either have failed to learn the laws that govern the building of wealth, or else you do not observe them. A part of all you earn is yours to keep. It should be not less than a tenth no matter how little you earn. It can be as much more as you can afford. Pay yourself first."

Safe from frivolous spending, the money will build up, and you'll hit your emergency fund baseline. From there, you keep saving, and you'll hit your opportunity fund threshold. Then, your strike number will begin to come into view, because your dollars are working more efficiently. You'll be covered in case of an emergency and now have the peace of mind to confidently buy your first house. The first one is always the hardest. Once you see the cash flow roll in, you'll want to buy more, and you'll get closer and closer to your strike number.

When you're just starting out, you can do this with as little as $200 to $300 a month. Start wherever you can and work up from there. Once you start to see your money grow, you'll get addicted to the process and start finding ways to put even more money into your emergency/opportunity fund every month.

If you need additional details about this strategy, reference the book *Live Your Life Insurance*.

THE LIE

The lie of this chapter is that qualified retirement plans are the best place to store capital.

When we're young, we're told, "Save your money for a rainy day." We're taught that we should save for savings' sake. That is not only boring but ineffective. It is much better to focus on liquidity than savings.

When you put your money into a qualified retirement plan, you're telling yourself you're saving, but you're really not. At best, you're investing, and at worst, you're speculating. People come straight out of college and start their first job, and they're told to pour their money into a 401(k) "savings plan."

A qualified retirement plan is not savings at all, as all of that money is locked up for decades. You can't use the money to repair the car, cover unexpected expenses, or pursue opportunities. You could technically be foreclosed on and kicked out of your home, and yet still have money in a qualified retirement plan. Your net worth would look just fine, but that wouldn't really help you, would it? You could be homeless, unable to get to work due to a broken-down car, but at least you have your 401(k) still, right? It's backwards. You certainly aren't free to invest in real estate when your money is tied up in a 401(k).

If you already have money in a 401(k), we're not suggesting you liquidate it and pay the penalties, though in some cases—perhaps if you hate your job and are looking to get out—that may be an option to consider. And if your employer offers a matching contribution, it can be worth it to take advantage of that. But a qualified retirement plan should *not* be your savings plan.

Another lie we're told about qualified retirement plans is that they're good for creating wealth. Surprise: they're not! Whole life insurance policies were created by entrepreneurs, but qualified retirement plans were created by the government and bureaucrats, and they were created for people who have jobs. They were not created for people who want to escape the nine-to-five environment and grow money outside of a traditional job.

Additionally, qualified retirement plans are retirement focused, and that's not helpful for people. The idea of retirement is a huge lie. Retirement doesn't work, and it never should have existed in the first place. Working yourself ragged until some arbitrary age is not good for you socially, physically, emotionally, psychologically, or financially. Various studies are starting to show the downsides of the retirement construct, and even the AARP has begun to shift the conversation, because people now realize you can't save money for thirty years and then try to live on it for another forty years. Except for a few very wealthy families, it's literally financially impossible. You would have to get a crazy rate of return to achieve the amount financial planners recommend saving for retirement.

There are tons of retirement calculators on the internet, but what we've discovered is that, while they might be mathematically correct, they may not be in line with your life. Our human lives are not mathematically designed. But if you want a place to start, we suggest going to *TruthConcepts.com/freetrial* where you can sign up for a free ten-day trial.

Experts say you can retire on 80 percent of your income, but that's not really realistic. A huge proportion of retirees are bored. They've spent the past thirty years with their nose to the grindstone, and now they have nothing to do. And what do bored people do? They spend more money than they should. When every day is a Saturday, you can't be expected to spend less than you did while working. So yes, you could theoretically retire on 80 percent of your income—if you tighten the purse springs and have no fun. That's no way to live life!

RETIREMENT IS NOT THE GOAL

Retirement is a dead idea, and it's not a good goal. A good goal is a strike number where you can spend your life doing what you love. The goal isn't *not* working but finding work that you can spend the rest of your life doing, because work and service to humanity is what gives people energy. Rather than *having* to go to work or being bored, with nothing to do, you get to go to work. You get to wake up each morning excited to start the day. You get to work mostly in the area of your Unique Ability®, as the concept is seen in the work of Dan Sullivan, founder of Strategic Coach®.

Yet despite the flaws of retirement, qualified retirement plans are purely focused on retirement and that mythical time frame of age fifty-nine and a half when you're finally allowed access to your money. And, you're also required, at age seventy and a half, to take the money out, whether you want to or not. Nowadays, you can be into your eighties, active, and still working because you love your job, but even though you're earning an income, you have to withdraw from your 401(k) plan or IRA because of your age.

In contrast, using whole life insurance opens opportunities. More whole life insurance gets you more real estate, which gets you more whole life insurance. The cash flow allows you to reach your strike number, which gets you more time to do what you want. It's an endless cycle that constantly grows your wealth—whole life insurance, real estate, whole life insurance, real estate—all with the freedom to live your life doing what you love.

This process is slow and steady, but it's also exciting and inspiring, because you can see your money working for you and see yourself getting closer to your strike number. In contrast, having your money sitting in a checking account somewhere gathering dust can create anxiety, making you feel as if you have to play catch-up. When your money is in a whole life insurance policy, you know you're earning a certain rate of return on it, and that eliminates the anxiety.

Remember: this is all about liquidity. You want cash-flowing money, not dead money. Whole life insurance gives you the liquidity and real estate gives you the cash flow. The two together enable you to invest in more real estate and anything else you'd like.

Chapter 3
EMBRACE A CASH-FLOW MINDSET

You can't eat equity.

—Anonymous

W hen most people think about creating wealth, they think about amassing a large amount of assets on a balance sheet and talking about their net worth. This mindset is flawed. Instead of thinking about accumulating numbers on a balance sheet, you need to think about accumulating assets that kick off cash flow. Bankers care about your net worth, but you should not. You should care about how much cash your assets are kicking off every month. Instead of focusing on *storing* money, you should be thinking about cash flow. You don't need $500,000 sitting in the bank, because it's really not sitting in the bank. You don't need a balance sheet that says you are worth half a million dollars in order to start living the life you want; instead, you need to accumulate assets that kick off cash, and you need that cash to equal your expenses every month. That's your strike number: the amount of money you need to live each month needs to equal the amount of money you collect monthly from the assets you own. Accumulating $1 million is a daunting task, but accumulating $1 million in cash-flowing assets is not that difficult.

A common misperception about real estate is that it's all about the HDTV model of flipping houses—you buy a house for x dollars, spend y to rehab it, and then sell it for x + y + $50,000, pocketing the profit. You can make money with this approach, but you will be a professional speculator. People who do this are not real estate investors; rather, they are building a business with systems. If you want to build wealth over time with real estate, flipping houses is not your goal. It is a full-time job and another business, one based on speculation. You can't count on it or build your life around it. You need to then invest that money in something that doesn't require so much time and isn't as subject to market volatility.

Relying too heavily on speculation is exactly what got everybody into so much trouble in 2008. People were flipping houses and making crazy amounts of money, but then as soon as the market turned, the banks stopped lending, and those same people took heavy losses. They were spectators who went from net worth based "real estate moguls" to bankrupt—houses foreclosed, cars repossessed, everything gone, virtually overnight.

On the other hand, those people who focused on accumulating properties that provided a cash flow survived the storm just fine. Their approach wasn't as flashy, and they weren't making huge lump sums, but when the market turned, they were able to continue quietly building their portfolios and their income stayed relatively stable.

We are not trying to discourage flipping properties, or say that those who do are bad business people. Speculation can be a valuable tool in your tool belt, but if it's your primary strategy, you'll be completely dependent on market cycles. That's simply too volatile, and it's not the strategy we are talking about. We want to eliminate as many variables as possible. When you're focused on cash flow, you'll establish the cash flow needed to survive the ups and downs that will inevitably occur in life.

YOU CAN'T EAT EQUITY

Jimmy's Experience Rehabbing Houses

I'm involved in an absolute disaster of a rehab right now. We originally bought a property two years ago as a good lease-option house, but then we thought, "The market is hot. Let's rehab the whole thing and see what we can do." In essence, we got greedy. We thought we would make $10,000 on the flip, but it's been two years, and I have $100,000 tied up in the house. While it's now worth $125,000, it has taken two years of time, anger, frustration, and dead capital. I need to liquidate the money and put it back into other projects.

Through this process, I learned I'm not a speculator. I'm horrible at it and I can't emotionally handle it. My team is built to deliver lease-option rental properties, not to play in the speculation market. There are definitely millionaires who make money flipping houses or day trading, but they're very rare. What we are suggesting is very different from speculating. Our investment strategy has the most likelihood of success with a very low downside and a low risk of ruin.

What I also learned is that I only look at my balance sheet when my banker forces me to. I love it. "You can't eat equity." I hear people all the time say, "I have a million-dollar portfolio." But, it's all on paper. I don't care what my balance sheet says in terms of my portfolio worth because the appraisals aren't very accurate. I think what something is actually worth is what someone can buy it from you for in thirty days. The true value of my portfolio is how much cash value it kicks to me every month.

You can't eat equity. You can't take your balance sheet to the grocery store and buy food. You can't pay for a car. You can't pay for your kids' college tuition with a balance sheet. You can't eat equity of real estate, you can't eat equity of a business, and you can't eat assets that don't produce cash flow. Cash flow is what pays my bills, takes care of my family, runs my team, and pays the interest to the lenders. If I could have had the $100,000 tied up in my flip working for me, I would have invested in ten more homes with a cash flow of $200 a month. That would have earned me $25,000 a year.

NET WORTH DOESN'T MATTER

Your net worth does not matter. You should not be trying to accumulate anything but cash flow each month. The only time you should be checking your net worth is when you have to speak to a banker and do taxes.

Yet basically every financial advisor out there is focused on clients' net worth. Some advisors will dig in and help with budgeting, but at the end of the day, people don't know how to convert net worth into cash flow for income. Stock jockeys used to use bonds, but bonds aren't safe anymore, so now clients are forced to try to create income off of the stock market, which is incredibly volatile. If you opt for this method, you're left with the financial channels burned into your TV screen, as you don't know what else to do but watch the numbers tick up and down, hoping that your stocks will increase enough that you can sell a few shares and take some income. Some people turn to annuities, which pay about 4 or 5 percent, but at that point, you've totally lost control of your money. You don't have access to your asset, and there's no income to fill the time in-between, as you wait for your annuity to pay out.

We live our whole lives based on monthly incomes and budgets, and then all of a sudden, we're expected to switch gears and think about building a big lump sum when that's not how people live life or spend money. It just doesn't make sense.

CASH FLOW IS KING

When you're focused on cash flow, it doesn't matter if the underlying value of the real estate goes up or down. All you need to concern yourself with is whether a property is putting money into your pocket every month or not. From an advisor's perspective, this approach is fantastic, because you set it and forget it. You don't have to continually shore up clients' confidence in the stock market and explain why something is up or down in a quarterly review.

Investing in this process is boring but effective, because clients don't need to check the numbers or worry about the stock market crashing. None of that is relevant. The real estate market could drop 50 percent tomorrow, and nothing would change for people using this cash-flow-focused process. They would still be making money from their portfolios, as they are not dependent on the outside variable of market forces. A crash could actually be great for such individuals, as they would be in a position to take advantage of the downturn in prices to purchase more properties. Rents can fluctuate but they don't fluctuate nearly as much as home values do. Sometimes in a downturn rents actually go up because there is a higher demand for rentals since people are no longer able to get a loan to purchase a home.

THE LIE

The lie of this chapter is that appreciation is the means to achieving financial freedom. Brainwashed by financial media, we've been led to believe that rich people are athletes, actors, and individuals like Warren Buffet who have a huge net worth. In reality, wealthy people are those whose assets kick off cash flow that equal or exceed their expenses.

For many, this idea goes counter to everything they believe. Just as people mistakenly see a glamour in flipping houses, there's a misled glamour of what it means to be wealthy. Truly rich people often fall into the millionaire-next-door classification, a designation defined in *The Millionaire Next Door: The Surprising Secrets of America's Wealthy* by Thomas J. Stanley.[7]

Getting wealthy is not about buying fabulously glamorous mansions with granite countertops that might be featured in Lifestyles of the Rich and Famous. It isn't about keeping up with the Joneses, what car you drive, or what house you live in. It's simply how much cash your assets kick off each month and if they equal your expenses. Once that amount of cash equals or exceeds your expenses, you are wealthy. You are financially independent, whether you have a job or not. That's it. Period. It doesn't matter what type of showerhead you install or whether you own a Lamborghini. This method isn't sexy. You won't be bragging to your friends about the world-class properties you own, but you will have cash-flowing properties that provide you with freedom.

There's also a glamour to appreciation. It's exciting to see a 12 percent return on something, but what happens next? Yes, you

---

7   Thomas, Stanley J., "Portrait of a Millionaire," In *The Millionaire Next Door: The Surprising Secrets of America's Wealthy*, pp. 9-11. Lanham, MD: Taylor Trade Publishing, 2016.

can find discounted deals on real estate that allow you to make a profit from flipping, but just like so many people in 2008, you could just as easily take a big loss, as appreciation is tied to market factors. Relying solely on appreciation is not a sound business model. The people who are skilled at this have in-depth market experience and need to make sure they don't get too overextended at any given time. You can make money in a rising tide, but as soon as the market shifts, you'll go from champagne showers to the poorhouse. The consistency of monthly cash flow is much more valuable than one-off appreciation. Plus, making money off of speculation in this way requires real market expertise, whereas anyone can establish a cash flow system.

Cash flow hides in plain sight. In economics, there is no aggregate way to track and measure cash flow in a month or year. Economists only talk about gross domestic product and increase or decrease of asset values, completely ignoring the cash flow that comes in and out of all assets and businesses. These numbers are easy to identify, measure, and graph out. There is no easy graph for cash flow, and so nobody pays attention to it. There's no way to calculate the aggregate amount of cash flow in the entire economy. The closest equivalent to cash flow on Wall Street would probably be dividends, but so few stocks actually pay dividends nowadays. Instead, everyone is chasing appreciation and completely ignoring what makes economies and markets work.

As yet another added bonus, real estate cash flow is as close to tax-advantaged income as you're going to get. Dividends are taxed at ordinary income rates, but cash flow from real estate is taxed at an incredibly low rate. Depreciation flow is valuable, but this isn't the book to get into that topic. Instead, pick up Tom Wheelwright's book, *Tax-Free Wealth*.

Once you save up enough money in your emergency/opportunity fund and convert to a cash-flow mindset, you're ready to actually make your first real estate deal, using leverage to buy.

Chapter 4
USE LEVERAGE TO BUY

*Give me a lever long enough and a fulcrum on which to place it,
and I shall move the world.*

—Archimedes

Now let's talk about a controversial subject and the rule of leverage in building wealth. Instead of buying real estate with all cash, you should use leverage to buy. Use the money you've saved up in your emergency/opportunity fund as a down payment on a property. You simply access this money by borrowing against your whole life insurance policy. Then you have one loan with a whole life insurance company and a second loan with the bank as a first mortgage. When you do this, you take advantage of the bank's money to pay for a good portion of your investment, thus increasing your personal rate of return or cash-on-cash return. The Real Estate Analysis calculators from Truth Concepts show the rate of return for a property value of $100,000 with a mortgage payment and without.

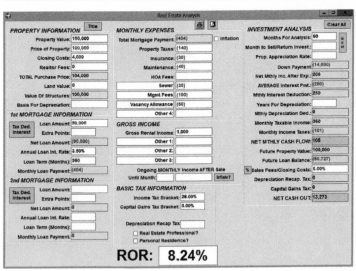

One of the unique traits of real estate is the ability to borrow money against it. No bank will even consider lending you money to buy stocks, nor will they give you a loan against your qualified retirement plan. That should be a red flag alerting you to the fact that qualified retirement plans can't truly be a great— much less secure—idea. Banks are in the business of loaning money to make money, and if they won't lend on something, it should tell you how they view those investment vehicles.

When you leverage your whole life insurance policy to buy real estate, you're not actually pulling money out of it; you're simply *borrowing* against it, just like when you take a loan on a house, you're borrowing against the value of the house. The life insurance company loans you their money, using your policy as collateral for the loan. Instead of using your own cash for the down payment, you are using the life insurance company's money. You pay interest to the life insurance company on the money you borrow, and all your money continues to accrue value inside of your policy, unaffected by the loan against it. This method is essentially a private loan that does not appear on your credit. The borrowed money is essentially cash that's placed in your account, so when you then use that money for a down payment, the bank has no concerns.

The interest owed on the money borrowed against your life insurance policy will be a small expense, but you can easily use the cash flow from your purchased property to pay back the life insurance loan. When the policy is fully paid back, you can borrow against it again for a down payment on another property.

BENEFITS OF USING LEVERAGE TO BUY

There are several benefits of leveraging your assets to purchase real estate. The most significant benefit is the ability to buy your first house much quicker than if you saved up to buy the house entirely in cash. The faster you buy your first house, the sooner your money begins to work for you, and the sooner you can take advantage of the benefits of owning real estate. Additionally, your cash-on-cash return will increase, because you're using other people's money.

Using leverage to buy also opens you up to more ways to make money besides just cash flow. For one, you get tax benefits, as you get to deduct the interest you're paying on the property as an expense. You—or, more accurately, your tenants—are also paying down your principal every month. While you can't access that principal until you refinance or sell the property, you are building value there. As a cherry on top, you have potential appreciation of the property.

Using leverage is also a way to be more antifragile. If you have $100,000 and buy a house with all cash, your capital is now tied up in that one property. If the tenant leaves, your cash flow immediately dries up. Even worse, if something happens to the property—say a fire or a flood—you're going to really be in trouble. If you have insurance, you won't lose everything, but you certainly won't be making money off the property for the months or years it can take to repair or rebuild. The better path is to split the $100,000 and put a 20 percent down payment on five different properties. You're no longer putting all your eggs in one basket, so there is less risk, and you have a safety net. If one tenant leaves or something happens to one property, you still have cash flow from the other four. Plus, when you purchase real estate with down payments, you can depreciate against all the money you borrow. If you buy just the one $100,000 house, you can probably depreciate only against $80,000, but if you buy the five houses, valued at a total of $500,000, you can depreciate against $400,000. Spreading your capital across properties thus provides greater tax savings as well. A video from Truth Concepts at https://www.youtube.com/watch?v=cgK_dOIesZo explains further the value of putting a second mortgage on homes using the cash value of your whole life insurance policy.

When you get a thirty-year loan to purchase a property, you'll end up paying the loan back with cheap dollars. We live in an inflationary environment. The dollars you have in your pocket today are much more valuable than the dollars thirty years from now because of inflation. Plus, with a loan, you lock in your principal and interest while having the potential for rent increases. In essence, your mortgage stays fixed while your rental income can increase.

MIDDLE CLASS WELFARE PAYMENTS

An additional benefit is that FHA loans for investment properties are the only subsidy available to the middle class. An FHA loan is a thirty-year loan with a fixed rate. No lender in their right mind would offer such a loan under normal circumstances, because there's too much volatility over thirty years to predict whether the loan will be a good use of capital. A lot can change in thirty years—just look at qualified retirement plans and the stock market, which became in vogue in the 1950s. They worked quite well between 1950 and 1990, providing good returns, but you can't rely on those forty years to predict the future. That forty-year period is a very small snippet of all of human history.

FHA loans exist only because the US government, wanting to promote home ownership, subsidizes the loans. They remove the risk from the lenders and put it on the government, which means us, the taxpayers. Because these loans are subsidized, they're like welfare payments, but they're intended for middle class individuals with w-2s and good credit. To get an FHA loan, you have to meet certain income and economic parameters just as you would to qualify for welfare. For lower-class welfare, you have to show a lack of income, and for this middle-class welfare, you have to show a certain amount of income. There are additional factors they take into consideration—including number of children and debt-to-income ratio. It's not another entrepreneur lending you the money but bureaucrats and regulators who dictate whether you are worthy for this loan or not.

Peter Schiff, economist, financial broker/dealer, and author, has said that in this unfair tax environment, it's a really bad idea to save up to purchase a house entirely in cash. If, for example, you want to buy a $100,000 house with cash, you really need to earn $135,000 in pre-tax income to do so, as you must account for your tax liability. Borrowed money is tax-free, you pay it back with your tenants' money, not your own, and you pay the bank back with devalued money over the thirty-year loan.

Members of the middle class are currently eligible for ten FHA loans, and married couples where both partners work are eligible for twenty. These limits could change, so take advantage of as many of these loans now, while you can. When the gravy train ends and you're no longer eligible for FHA loans, you enter into a new risk category. You will then have to use other strategies to purchase homes: getting private money loans, commercial loans with balloons, or nonrecourse loans with more money down.

Some of you may be wondering at this point, *Is this a moral dilemma? Am I perpetuating the welfare system if I use these loans?* In a perfect world, a libertarian utopia, we would not have the Federal Reserve or FHA financing. We would be backed by the gold standard, and our currency would be sound. But until that environment exists, there's no point in taking the woe-is-me victim mentality, lamenting over how the big bad government takes your money and there's nothing you can do about it. Taking advantage of FHA loans is what you can do about it. The government is ruining the value of the dollar, causing you to lose money to inflation; when you use FHA loans, you are using the government's very tool of inflation against them. You make your money back at their expense. You can also look at FHA loans as borrowing back what you've already paid in taxes.

At the end of the day, it's all about personal economic liberty, personal autonomy. If you want to achieve that, FHA loans are the most efficient way to do it. All you can worry about is yourself. You can't control the greater scheme, so you should work to create your own personal financial freedom, bringing the sphere of control back into your own world as much as possible.

DISCOVERING THE FIFTEEN-YEAR LOAN IS A HORRIBLE IDEA

Kim Discovers the Typical Advice Is Misguided

I grew up a banker and was taught to prepay mortgages. Throughout the late 1980s, I told all my clients—even my parents—to get fifteen-year mortgages and to prepay, because that's what I thought was best.

In the late 1990s, I met my husband, Todd, and he provided me the proof that thirty-year mortgages were more efficient. I really struggled with this idea and disagreed vehemently initially, as it went against everything I had learned. I had a great assistant at the time, and he helped me crunch all the numbers. Using a loan-analysis calculator, a cash-flow calculator, and about twenty different financial calculators, he proved to me over and over again that a thirty-year mortgage was better than a fifteen-year mortgage. With the layers of proof, it finally sunk in for me that getting a fifteen-year mortgage and prepaying was a terrible idea.

I felt absolutely horrible. I went to my parents and had them stop prepaying. That was an easy fix. Refinancing them back to a thirty-year mortgage was not as easy. We eventually did, but it took time. Thankfully, my parents were pretty forgiving and ended up fine financially, but this was nonetheless a very painful lesson for me to learn.

THE CREATION OF TRUTH CONCEPTS

Truth Concepts was created in order to get all the truth about a particular financial decision on a level playing field. Advisors and individuals often look at their personal finances in a vacuum. They forget the time value of money and they forget to look at equal time frames. An interest rate has to be applied to the monetary calculations after even one day. The payments must be at interest because cash has value and people forget that. They think their $100,000 has no value in an account, but it does. You can't compare a fifteen-year mortgage over fifteen years to a thirty-year mortgage over thirty years. You have to have the same time frame but everyone does it incorrectly. The Truth Concepts' calculators take into account all of it—including the interest rate, cost of money, time frame, value of the dollar, etc. It's incredibly valuable to determine the value on paper. A property and the resulting spreadsheet can look amazing, but it doesn't always translate to other details like the location and neighborhood of the property. Data is like the bumpers on the bowling alley when you play with your children. It's crucial that you weigh all aspects.

If you need further understanding of this concept, please take the time to read the Weighing Your Mortgage Options excerpt in the appendix before continuing!

THEY ARE ALL THE SAME

It is true that you will pay less interest on a fifteen-year mortgage than a thirty-year mortgage, but less interest does not necessarily mean less cost, especially considering the deductibility of interest. Even if you couldn't deduct interest, a thirty-year mortgage is still better. If a thirty-year fixed mortgage is priced at 4 percent, the fifteen-year fixed rate will be around 3.75 percent. For the fifteen-year mortgage to equal the total cost of the thirty-year mortgage, that rate would need to be as low as 2.25 percent.

People become misguided because they want to compare different time frames. Comparing a fifteen-year mortgage over fifteen years to a thirty-year mortgage over thirty years is not valid. Either you should compare both of them over fifteen years or both of them over thirty years, but you can't use different time frames for each. People also tend to compare different interest rates. As in any scientific environment, you can only change one variable at a time if you want to get an accurate result. People who argue that fifteen-year mortgages are better tend to change two or three things at a time and then make a comparison, which presents skewed findings.

If a fifteen-year mortgage is truly better than a thirty-year mortgage, than an all-cash payment would be even better, right?

Not so. In fact, as proved with a laborious process using the Truth Concepts' calculators, if the interest rates are the same, the opportunity cost (what else you can do with the money) is factored in, and the three options are compared over thirty years, then they are all the same. This can be a hard concept to wrap your mind around, but it is crucial to understand.

WHY A LONGER MORTGAGE IS BETTER

When you're investing in real estate, a thirty-year mortgage is best in order to optimize cash flow. Choosing a fifteen-year mortgage nullifies the cash flow that you would get with a thirty-year mortgage. Instead of getting money out of a property, you're putting money in. A house that was supposed to be an asset becomes a liability.

When you opt for a shorter mortgage, you also make the assumption that you can't earn more with your money than the interest you're paying. If you're paying 4 percent interest to the bank and choose a fifteen-year loan to save on interest, you're basically saying that you can't make any more than that 4 percent, which is a limited mindset. There are plenty of real estate investments available that will earn more than that. Even putting your money into a whole life insurance policy can possibly give you a higher return than that.

Essentially, if you choose a fifteen-year mortgage, you're tying your money up in the house. Yes, you pay your principal down faster, but what good does that do you? The principal is inaccessible until you sell or refinance the house. Remember: you can't eat equity. If you experience a liquidity crunch on a personal level, like during the 2008 crash, you will be stuck without cash flow, unable to afford your mortgage payments, and unable to sell or refinance the home. You're back in the scarcity mindset.

With a fifteen-year mortgage, you delay to the future what you could be realizing today. Instead of waiting for a larger cash flow in fifteen years when the house is paid, it's better to get a smaller cash flow consistently across the course of a thirty-year mortgage.

Now, if you have the ability to raise private capital and can get interest-only loans, great—that is the most ideal way to maximize cash flow. But for most people, the closest option to an interest-only loan is to get a thirty-year, fixed-rate loan.

Banks want you to get a fifteen-year mortgage because you're increasing their cash flow. They get a higher monthly payment while holding the same value as collateral. Whether you owe $1,000 or $50,000 on a property, if the house is worth $100,000, they are just as secure. When you prepay your principal, you simply increase the bank's equity in the deal if they were to take the property back.

You give up control and lower the bank's risk while simultaneously increasing your own risk. Let's say you have a fifteen-year mortgage and have paid off 90 percent of the principal on the property. You run into a liquidity crunch, and the bank forecloses. You lose all the money you put into the property. If instead you have a thirty-year mortgage, you may have only paid down 5 percent of the principal, and so you wouldn't lose as much money. The more principal you pay down, the higher your risk goes, until you completely pay off the house.

When you choose a thirty-year mortgage, you can invest the liquidity into other opportunities. You can put the money you're saving into your whole life insurance policy, and once your emergency/opportunity fund builds back up, you can put a down payment on another house. Rinse and repeat. Instead of focusing on paying off only one house, you're focused on how to build your portfolio, adding more cash-flowing assets. Even if you're just going to let your money sit, you'll pay that first house off faster by putting the money into your whole life insurance policy rather than by putting it into the walls of the house.

The concept of paying off a house quickly is tied to the myth of the middle class and retirement. People want to pay off their mortgages so they don't have that payment to worry about in retirement. But even when you have a paid-off house, it doesn't do anything for you. It is still not a cash-flowing asset. It's a liability. You still owe taxes on it, you still have to pay maintenance expenses, and a significant amount of liquidity is locked inside the walls of the house. In the past, people would buy a home, stay put, and easily have it paid off in thirty years. But now, people move so often and refinance for various reasons, like putting a kid through school, that tons of people in their fifties and sixties are nowhere near getting their thirty-year mortgage paid off. So you shouldn't be worried about trying to pay off a house just for retirement purposes.

THE LIE

The lie of this chapter is that all debt is bad.

A big aspect of this lie is a false equivalency of two very different things: being in debt and having debt. Being in debt means you will have to trade time for money to pay that debt off. Having debt means that you have debt backed by cash-flowing assets that the asset pays off, not your labor. It is choosing to have some liabilities but even-greater assets—you own more than you owe. You are choosing to have debt. Being in debt, on the other hand, is when you owe more than you own. For example, when you graduate from college and have $70,000 in student loans, $20,000 on your credit card, and no assets, you don't just have debt; you are *in* debt. Being *in* debt is not good, but *having* debt is a totally different ball game.

Debt is a tool. It can be good or bad depending on how you use it. Religious and cultural connotations often make the subject of debt taboo. In the Middle Ages, the church outlawed usury for about five hundred years, and that action was more harmful to human development than believing the sun revolved around the earth. A mindset that debt is inherently bad will hold you back. Do you want a big pile of cash sitting in a bank doing nothing, or do you want cash-flowing assets?

Understanding time preference can help you shift your perspective of debt. Children have a high time preference. If you give children money, they will usually spend it all immediately on candy and junk. They want what they want when they want it. They have no ability to see and plan for the future. Spending for consumption—spending money on cars, vacations, ball games, and so on—is also a sign of high time preference. On the other hand, the accumulation of liquidity inside your whole life insurance policy indicates you have lowered your time preference.

Eugen von Böhm-Bawerk, a famous economist who helped create the Austrian School, discusses this time disconnect in *Capital and Interest*.[8] Similarly, Frédéric Bastiat also argues that humans overvalue consumption today (the seen) and undervalue consumption tomorrow (the unseen).

The time disconnect is critical to understanding debt's role in investing. The rate of interest you pay on borrowed capital is the cost you are willing to pay for a higher time preference. Interest is a line-item cost as opposed to this evil enigma that religious organizations and people like Dave Ramsey rail against. Once you break debt and interest down to dollars and cents, they lose their ability to scare people.

There are varying levels of risk associated with each source of debt. The lower the risk of ruin, the better the debt source is. Of course, there's no such thing as zero-risk debt, but there are acceptable forms of risk and acceptable forms of debt.

Not all debt is equal.

---

8   von Böhm-Bawerk, Eugen, *Capital and Interest: A Critical History of Economic Theory*. Translated by William Smart, M.A.. New York: Brentano's, 1922.

Type of Loan	Risk of Ruin and Recourse
Loan Shark	Risk of ruin is physical harm. No risk to your credit report though!
Payday Loan	High compounding interest and possible risk to your credit report.
Consumer Credit Card	High compounding debt and your credit score can be destroyed.
Zero Percent Interest Business Cards	High compounding interest after the teaser rate. It can ruin your business credit score, but can't impact your personal credit.
Commercial Bank Loan	Interest rate, balloons, potential rate hikes, and the loans are still recourse. Personal guarantees put personal assets at stake.
Non-Recourse Commercial Bank Loans	There's a higher down payment and you have a greater risk to lose the capital you already put into it. Your exposure is limited to the dollars you put into the down payment.
Private or Hard Money Loans	The interest rate is a little higher, but there's no risk to personal assets or your credit report.
Conventional Mortgage Backed by Real Estate	Very little risk. Fixed rate, no balloons. There is personal recourse but the fixed rate for thirty years is almost free money with inflation.
Private Money Backed by Asset	This is an advanced concept where the loan is interest-only which maximizes cash flow. Debt to a whole life insurance company also falls in this level because it is non-recourse and the company can only go after the asset.

Breaking debt and interest down in this way shows the difference between good debt that comes with acceptable risk and bad debt that comes with too high of a risk. For example, we would not go to a loan shark or use a credit card to buy a property, because the interest would kill all our cash flow, and the risk of physical harm from the loan shark would not make the gain on buying the house acceptable!

Cash sitting in a savings account or even a whole life insurance policy doesn't do much for you unless that cash interweaves with assets and gains velocity. Our wealth-creation system coupling real estate and whole life insurance works so well because the money is gaining velocity, and the same dollars are interweaving themselves and kicking off cash flow in several different assets.

Chapter 5
PARTNER WITH OPERATORS

Unique Ability®, by definition, is the essence of what you love to do and do best. It's your own set of natural talents and the passion that fuels you to contribute in the ways that most motivate you. When articulated, it describes the "you" that makes you who you are.

—Dan Sullivan

Remember that your ultimate goal is to create cash flow from assets in order to provide more freedom in your life. If you work full-time and also try to manage your own properties, something that is meant to be automated will quickly turn into another low-paying job. Your goal is to be a real estate investor, not a property manager. You want to accumulate cash-flowing assets, not work another job, so you're going to have to partner and work with other operators.

In this context, an operator is a full-time real estate investor who has the team, systems, and processes to ensure that your property cash flows. Operators are different from aggregators. Operators own their own properties in addition to managing properties for others, whereas aggregators are marketers and salespeople who don't personally own any of their own properties. Aggregators serve a purpose, but let's cut out the middleman. Go to the person who knows the ins and outs of the business and is tied to the longevity of the process.

Rather than becoming a full-time real estate investor, you can use a turnkey management company. Turnkey management companies are beneficial because they have systems, processes, and know-how to take a property and turn it into a cash-flowing asset. At Vreeland Capital, we add several new houses to our system each month. At the time of this writing, we own 160 of our own properties, so adding six or seven more isn't a big deal; it only expands our efficiency. When we first started, we owned between one and fifty properties, and the property management was hellacious and inefficient. It's like having children. Going from zero kids to one kid is a huge change and incredibly difficult. By the time you have your fourth kid, though, it's a piece of cake, because you are experienced and have systems in place.

Most people's biggest objection to getting into real estate investing is not having the time or know-how. The turnkey companies and operators provide you with that know-how and time. You are strictly an investor; you're not signing up for a second job.

When you have under fifty properties, you don't have the experience or systems to manage them effectively. You can't afford to pay for technology and staff, so you must deal with all the minutiae yourself. It is much more efficient if you can partner with a management company who *can afford them.*

THE BENEFITS OF PARTNERSHIP

Jimmy Struggles to Do It All Himself
and Sees Others Make the Same Mistake

When I was in medical sales, I owned six properties, and I managed them myself. At times, I had to put doctors on hold to talk to tenants. I would lose out on $20,000 calls to take care of $20 leaky faucets. It didn't make any sense.

Everyone wants to get their hands dirty initially. They want to find, buy, and manage properties all by themselves. But then life happens. They get busy, and they're pulled back into work, family, and community commitments. Six months down the line, they still haven't bought even one house and are no further along in their financial and real estate goals.

At Vreeland Capital, people often start out wanting to apply our system in their own neighborhoods. We've even had friends who initially wanted to do it all on their own. Eventually, almost everyone realizes utilizing us as turnkey operators is much easier. All they have to do is say they want a house, and we find one that meets their needs in St. Louis. We take care of all the management for a percentage of the rental income, while they keep doing what they've always done. They can stay in their job and not take on another job of real estate investor. They're like the CEO of a company with us as the COO.

LEVERAGING OTHERS' ABILITIES

We have both been mentored by Dan Sullivan, 10x Coach and founder of the Strategic Coach® program, and his concept of Unique Ability® has influenced us greatly. You can learn more by reading his book *Unique Ability 2.0: Discovery-Define Your Best Self.*

Unique Ability® is the idea that each person has work that they love and are passionate about. They are always interested in improving it, and that's different than work that they just like. We constantly apply the concept to every personal relationship, business relationship, and business partnership that we engage in. We would all be happier if we could take advantage of others' Unique Abilities® while devoting our time to performing our own Unique Abilities®. Thinking about our own Unique Ability® allows us to peel back the layers to get clearer on the work that we love. We are happier, our money works more efficiently, and our family and friends benefit from the results.

This idea relates to the economic concept of comparative advantage, which states that you shouldn't try to do everything. If you're a doctor, you shouldn't act as a receptionist as well. Even if you're two times more efficient than the current receptionist, you're one hundred times a better doctor, so you should dedicate your time to that career. Everyone has a comparative advantage, and so everybody should have a job they are suited for. *Not a Zero-Sum Game: The Paradox of Exchange*, a book on economy by Manuel F. Ayau, perfectly illustrates this point.

We're not telling you to quit your job to solely invest in real estate and whole life insurance, though that is eventually possible, if that's what you want to do. You can continue to lead your life, playing to your Unique Ability®, while still growing wealth through real estate and whole life insurance. This approach is the fastest and most efficient way to grow wealth, and it allows you to continue to pursue your passion and have fun. It is your Unique Ability®, not your rental portfolio and whole life insurance policies, that is the catalyst to your wealth. Your rentals and policies are simply where you sustain and grow your wealth.

When you begin investing in real estate, you're going to pay in one capacity or another. Either you pay a management fee to gain another's experience, or you pay through the school of hard knocks. If you don't know the right neighborhoods or the right types of homes to buy, you could end up losing money. Due to that negative experience, you could even lose the desire to own real estate at all. Many people who try to do everything themselves end up giving up on real estate before they figure out how to make it work for them. There's a steep learning curve, and there's only so much you can learn from reading books and taking courses. After that, it comes down to experience gained from actually dealing with the various problems that can arise.

At Vreeland Capital, we have many years of experience and several hundred deals under our belts, but for our first twenty deals, we faced many difficulties and made a lot of mistakes. A lot of properties look good on paper. You calculate the money needed to purchase the house and rehab it, and you can determine the likely rents based upon rental comps. These figures determine your expected cash flow. Unfortunately, there are factors you must consider that don't always show up on paper.

In every town there are certain dividing lines between good and bad areas. Sometimes the line can even run down the middle of the street, with one side good and one side bad. You can only learn about these invisible boundaries with time and experience, as there's only so much due diligence you can do by walking or driving by a house. Often, it takes buying homes in the wrong neighborhood to learn to never buy there again.

For a while, we had a house on Bridge Row that looked great on paper. Bridge Row is a decent area. The problem was the house was right next to some train tracks, and the only place to cross over the tracks for a mile in either direction was right in front of the house. Every day, kids walked by the house after school so they could cross the tracks. Being mischievous teenagers with nothing better to do, they often threw rocks at the windows of the house. We ended up having to replace the windows three or four times. They kept getting busted out. Constantly replacing the windows killed the cash flow, and we finally decided to cut our losses and sell the house.

Some of our best deals are in that zip code, but that specific property was a disaster. It can happen anywhere. You can have streets that are extremely profitable, but if you go two blocks in either direction, it doesn't work anymore. The houses are a pain to manage and a pain to make money on. When you partner with an operator, you gain their expertise and knowledge to hopefully avoid disaster properties.

WHAT IT TAKES TO DO IT ALONE

Finding a House

One of the key components of real estate is identifying which neighborhood will maximize cash flow while simultaneously reducing management issues. Some real estate investors try to use a stock market analyst approach to invest in real estate. For all I know, it works, because there are several hedge funds right now trying to get institutional money onto Main Street. And for the guys who are working on Main Street, we are highly suspicious that this is big, dumb money coming into our market. They look at various macroeconomic indicators in different markets and make decisions based on that information. You can use macroeconomic indicators as a veto analysis, but it doesn't work to look at a map and choose a property. This approach simply doesn't work. Those indicators are just noise. Real, everyday experience is needed.

Let's say you can buy a 1,200 square foot house for $90,000 and expect to earn $1,200 in rent each month. If you moved that exact same house—same age, same architecture—into a neighborhood with higher property values, you could make $1,500 in rent, but the house would cost $200,000. Paying more than twice as much to get only $300 extra per month doesn't make sense. From a cash flow perspective, it's much better to purchase two houses in the first neighborhood than one house in the second one, even if it has a higher potential for appreciation. As we already discussed, appreciation is a riskier model that does not maximize cash flow.

Consider this rate of return and property evaluation for a property located on Monks Street.

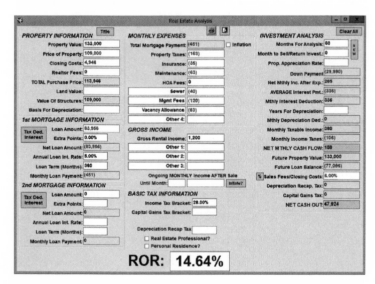

Property Evaluation Form: 2041 Monks Hollow Dr 63031

Key Performance Indicators

Cash on Cash Return	14.6%	Gross Rent Multiplier	6.9	CoC Breakeven (Yrs)	6.9
Expense Ratio	40%	Rent to Value	1.2%	1st Cash Out Refi (Yrs)	
Price/Sq Ft	88.3	Cap Rate	9%	1st Cash Out Refi ($)	

General Property Information		Property Operations Information			Key Metrics Requirements		
Property Values		**Rental Assumptions**			**Absolute Ratios**	Min	Target
Zestimate	133,809	Units	1		Cash on Cash	8.0%	10.0%
Purchase Price	100,000						
Tenant Purchase Price	109,900	Rents	1,200		GRM	10	8
Sq ft	1,133	Other Income	-		Expense Ratio	30%	40%
		Total Potential Income	1,200		Rent to Value	0.8%	1.2%
Finanacing Information					Cap Rate	8%	10%
Down Payment (%)	20%	**Known Expenses (Monthly)**					
Interest Rate	5.00%	Property Taxes	163	14%	Projections		
Loan Term (Yrs)	30	Insurance	35	3%	Cash Out		70%
Monthly Payment	451	Sewer	40	3%			
Annual Payment	5,408	Management Fees	120	10%		Market	Target
Fixed/Variable	Fixed	Other 1	-	0%	Demographic Ratios	Average	Discount
Closing Costs (%)	4.50%	Other 2	-	0%	Price/Sq Ft	80	10%
Closing Costs ($)	4,946	Other 3	-	0%			
		Total Known Expenses	358	30%			
Cash Requirements							
Loan Amount	83,956	**Estimated Expenses (Monthly)**					
Down Payment ($)	20,989	Vacancy Allowance	63	5%			
Reserves	901.39	Maintenance Allowance	63	5%			
Renovations		Other 1	-	0%			
Total Cash Required	21,890	Other 2	-	0%			
		Other 3	-	0%			
Future Assumptions		Total Est Expenses	125	10%			
Appreciation Rate	2.0%						
Inflation Rate	2.0%	LT Cash Flow Adjustment		40%			
Closing Costs	3.0%						
Refi Costs	1.0%	Net Operating Income	717	60%			
		Net Cash Flow	266	22%			

*Grey cells represent formulas that should not be altered or have values entered directly.

In the opposite direction, you could buy a house in a war zone, low-income neighborhood for $40,000 and expect $700 in monthly rent. While you could technically get more cash flow in such a neighborhood, you're going to have higher vacancy, more turnover, and more vandalism, like the house on Bridge Row. These neighborhoods are typically composed entirely of rentals. In general, the people there won't have as much pride in ownership, and they won't be taking care of the properties. They will be difficult to manage, and due to all the increased expenses, you're never going to end up collecting what you expect on houses in these neighborhoods. We know these prices might sound made up or impossible to many people but, in our market of St. Louis and several areas in the Midwest, they are indeed a reality.

You need to find a balance between the extremes.

Once you find the right neighborhood, you will need to look at ten to twenty properties a week until you find the one that's right. You will need to find a realtor and then spend your weekends walking through tons of houses. Then you have to start making offers, most of which won't be accepted. Instead, you could leverage a turnkey provider's team who understands this and looks at thousands of homes every year.

Managing a Rehab

The houses that work well for this method always require repairs. The reason we can acquire them at a below-market price is because we are able to do the repairs. Otherwise, you have to pay top dollar for the house and won't be able to maximize your cash flow. Once you get an offer accepted and buy a house, you begin the work of rehabbing it. This involves hiring a contractor, building a scope for the house, creating an estimate, collecting bids, and negotiating pricing. Since you're not a volume buyer, you won't be able to get a great deal in the negotiation. On the other hand, turnkey providers spend $30,000 to $40,000 a week on rehabs, so they have a lot of leverage in negotiations. Contractors want to work with them and are willing to give more favorable pricing on supplies than they would give a one-off buyer.

Many real estate DIYers make the mistake of over improving their rental properties. They put in granite countertops and nice mosaic tile. These improvements look nice, but they provide only marginal increase in extra rent compared to the cost of the house. For each incremental dollar you're paying in repairs, you're not necessarily going to make that money back in actual income on the property. It's similar to the fact that you don't want the more expensive house in a better neighborhood. At Vreeland Capital, we make cost-effective repairs based upon what we know will attract quality tenants.

It took twenty to thirty properties and several years' worth of trial and error for us to learn which neighborhoods to buy in; which types of houses to buy, from square footage to layout; and which types of repairs to make. Unless you're operating in the market every day getting instant feedback, you won't learn all these little details fast enough to gain momentum. Plus, you most likely won't get the really great deals, as those tend to be snatched up by the volume operators in town.

Working with Tenants

Once you buy and rehab a house, then there are the ongoing tasks that come with owning a property. First, you have to find a tenant. You need to take pictures and market the home. Once the phone rings with calls from potential tenants, you have to show the property. You'll drive to the property to meet people and also deal with no-shows, which are very common in the rental business. Then, when you find people who are interested, you will get completed applications and screen them to determine who will be a good tenant long term. Finally, after picking a tenant, you will handle the lease and all the required documentation.

There's a lot of minutiae involved in putting together a single rental deal, and if you don't have a system in place, it can be very time consuming. Turnkey providers have a team of people who do all of these various tasks. We've both done it all on our own before, and it was, quite frankly, miserable.

After the tenant is placed, the work doesn't end. You still have to manage the property. If something needs to be repaired, you'll have to hire someone to take care of it or do it yourself. One of the interesting aspects of the Vreeland Capital model is that in our leases the tenant is responsible for the majority of ongoing repairs and maintenance. We still take care of big repairs—like if a huge storm rips the roof off of a property—but the tenant handles the tiny annoying repairs, like drippy faucets and circuit breaker issues.

You will also have to deal with bad tenants. The process to evict can be daunting and frustrating. If you're partnered with a management company, they will handle everything—the collections, phone calls with the tenant, and coordination with an eviction attorney. If you're on your own, all of those tasks fall on you. If you don't know what you're doing and make one small mistake, like not filling the various paperwork out correctly, it can take six months or more to get a bad tenant evicted. If you're working with an operator, you might never deal with bad tenants in the first place due to experienced screening. But if you do run into a bad tenant, the operator has the systems and processes in place to evict that tenant quickly and put a new tenant in place.

Professional tenants—people who know the ins and outs of the eviction process and who know how to game the system—typically look for single operators and newbies. They look for people who are easy to take advantage of, people who are inexperienced and don't have the systems in place to handle evictions quickly. A professional tenant will scrape together enough money for the security deposit and first month's rent, and then the next month, when rent is due, they don't pay. Most mom-and-pop and first-time landlords haven't learned to be tough managers, so they often wait another month before even starting the eviction process. By the time they finally get the professional tenant out, they've lost many months of income on the property.

Unless you're naturally an extremely firm negotiator, chances are that you're going to be way too easy on your tenants. It's a business, and you have to constantly train your tenants on how the system works. You need to have a policy and repercussions if rent is not paid on time, and you need to enforce it. We've heard every possible story for why the rent isn't going to be paid on time. Once you hear so many stories, you become numb to them. There's always going to be a story. At the end of the day, your job is to protect the income of the property.

This absolutely requires a team on every front. If you love your job…or even if you don't…what you currently do to make income is serving you. It's not necessary to quit your job and become a full-time real estate investor or whole life insurance salesman to execute this strategy.

Kim Tries Her Hand at Being an Excel Millionaire

My husband and I owned a small apartment building in a tiny town in Texas, and it ended up being a disaster. This is an example of what Jimmy talked about where the pro forma looks good, but the tenants inside the neighborhood will not support the numbers. A bunch of thieves broke in and tore apart the walls to steal the copper piping. My husband was gone at the time, so when the police called about the break-in, I had to handle it. I went over to the property, and a police officer on the scene told me to stay in my car because they never know what they will find in situations like this.

The officers pulled their guns and converged on the building, crouched down. It was in the middle of the day, and as I watched all of this, sitting in my car in my business attire, I thought, *Oh my gosh, I'm in the wrong place. Get me out of here.*

We got rid of that building as quickly as we could. It was not our Unique Ability® to own apartment buildings. Our town was so small geographically that we couldn't get the leverage that Vreeland Capital gets by owning a large number of properties.

After that, I was turned off of real estate. It's easy to mentally understand the benefits of property ownership and to pencil out the cash flow, but the physical act of owning the real estate—of dealing with phone calls and minutiae and even calls from the police—is completely different. We even had a property manager, yet sometimes as an owner, you are forced to get involved.

Even in less extreme cases, the everyday physical tasks of real estate ownership can be draining. My husband and I owned another property, an office building, that had an onsite manager, and I still received calls every single day to make a decision or give final approval. I frequently got frustrated and would roll my eyes, thinking, *Why am I dealing with this?* These things simply aren't part of my Unique Ability®. For people who do have the appropriate Unique Abilities®, they should make their own deals and maybe even manage and operate their own properties. But people like me should instead partner with operators. That way, the involvement is financial but not physical.

I'm now an investor with Vreeland Capital. I basically spent five minutes on the phone setting up the deal, and then I emailed my bookkeeper to have her move the money to the escrow account. I can't even tell you what the address of the house I'm invested in is, but every month checks show up. I tried the DIY approach and hated it. My Unique Abilities® were better spent elsewhere, and so I abandoned the approach.

Jimmy Realizes the Worth of a Team

When I first started working in real estate, I would wake up, check Craig's List and Zillow, put in offers myself, work with the real estate agent, pay for it myself, find tenants on my own, and attempt to manage the property—all while working in medical sales. On one line, I'd be speaking to a doctor about medical devices, and on the other line, I'd be negotiating with a tenant who refused to pay rent. It was completely irrational to do this without a team. I now have a team of fifteen people, each working as close to their Unique Ability® as possible.

LEASE OPTIONS VS. TRADITIONAL RENTING

Part of the uniqueness of the Vreeland Capital model is that we do lease options on our properties as opposed to regular rentals. This way, we get tenants who have home ownership mentality. They want to buy a house, but there's something currently preventing them from doing so. Typically, it's a credit issue, but it could also be that they don't have enough saved up for a down payment. They might be self-employed business owners who don't have enough taxable income to qualify for a traditional mortgage.

Lease-option tenants have more skin in the game and pride in taking care of the property. Their security deposits are typically more than a standard rental, and they aren't willing to walk away from it, so they pay the rent on time and abide by the contracts. They take better care of the property because long term they want to be a homeowner and buy the home. Fewer issues come up with the property, and there is less wear and tear. Many times people actually improve the house by

installing tile flooring or painting the rooms. They know they're going to buy it someday, so they want to take care of it.

Lease option is a simple free-market and underused solution. The reason I like lease option is because I want to do business with potential homeowners who actually want to improve their current situation. I don't necessarily want to work with professional tenants. I serve an underserved market, where many of our tenants cannot qualify for conventional financing. We give them a two-year reprieve to work with us, live in a home, and we help them fix their credit so they can enter into the middle class by getting their home financed.

THE LIE

The lie of this chapter is that investing in real estate has to take a lot of time for the buyer.

Real estate investing does not take a lot of time. If you want to do it all yourself, then yes, it will be very time consuming for you. However, if you choose to take advantage of others' Unique Abilities®, you can dedicate minimal time and still reap the benefits.

Essentially, real estate investing does take a lot of time, but it doesn't have to take a lot of time for *you*. If you partner with an experienced operator that already has the necessary systems, processes, and people in place, they will handle just about everything for you. The core of this lie stems from the real estate investment education industry, which shows you the high side of investing in real estate, but does not bring you to the reality that you need to be able to be an acquisitioner, rehabber, leasing agent, property manager, and financier. For most people, it's much better to work with an operator instead.

OPERATOR VS. EXPERT VS. MARKETER/SALESPERSON

The main difference between operators and both experts and marketers is that operators have skin in the game. They share the same risk as you.

Experts tend to be steeped in academia. They don't have their boots on the ground, and they don't roll up their sleeves and do the nitty-gritty work. An operator, on the other hand, has real-world experience and has learned real-world lessons. As a result, operators are more open to change. As leaders in our industry, we are constantly refining, changing, and bettering our businesses. We benefit from our constant evolution and adaptation, but the people who partner with us benefit as well.

Peter Diamandis, an engineer, physician, and entrepreneur known for his book, *Abundance: The Future Is Better Than You Think*, says that experts are people who don't want to change.[9] If we were only thought leaders, if we just wrote books about concepts and didn't actually work in these industries, we would not have learned as much and would not be as effective. Whatever

9 Diamandis, Peter. *Abundance: The Future Is Better Than You Think*. 1st Free Press hardcover edition. New York: Free Press, 2012.

the market throws at any of us, we can handle it, because we're constantly adapting and improving.

Salespeople and marketers get a bad rap—almost as bad as whole life insurance agents, realtors, and ambulance-chasing attorneys—but nothing in this world gets done until something is sold. We consider ourselves salespeople and marketers, but we are also operators currently in our own profession. And our goal is just trying to get people to open their minds. A book cannot sell you; it can only get you to open your mind.

Just as with the discussion of Unique Abilities®, it's not that one or the other—salesperson and operator—is better. If you are leveraging not only money but time, systems, technology, and Unique Ability®, you will perform exponentially better. Instead of $1+1=2$, it's $1+1=11$. Just beware that you're working with an operator and salesperson, not an aggregator.

As Yogi Berra said, "In theory there is no difference between theory and practice, but in practice there is."

WHAT NEXT?

Now that you understand what it takes to close just one deal, and that you need a team, how does this actually build your wealth over the long term? It's not worth learning this system if you're going to do it once! A single property isn't enough to provide financial freedom, so once you've made your first real estate deal, it's time to repeat the process.

Chapter 6

RINSE AND REPEAT AND EXPAND

Do not bury money into the walls of your house.

—Kim Butler

Your first real estate deal will be the hardest. Once you make that first deal, you don't need to reinvent the wheel. You simply need to repeat the process again, over and over, until you're financially free. By doing this, you will build the velocity of your money and add fuel to the whole process. It's simple but not easy, and each property will allow you to grow as an investor.

BUILDING VELOCITY

In typical financial planning, money gets stuck. The advice— investing in a 401(k) and a 529 plan and sinking money into a home through a too-large down payment and mortgage prepayment—causes money to die. You want your money to move and work for you. When you build velocity of money, your money moves *through* assets. As we've discussed before, an asset is anything you buy that kicks off cash flow. Whole life insurance policies and real estate are fine by themselves, but when you combine the two products, you get an exponential impact—you get velocity. You're not just putting your money *into* those products but *through* them. It is your strategy that gets the money to move assets.

When it comes to velocity, whole life insurance and real estate have worked together in this antifragile manner for over 200 years. Once you get your first property, you can use the cash flow from that house to pay back your whole life insurance policy loan. Then you can use the cash value that keeps building up in that policy for a down payment on a second property. Now you have even more cash flow, which becomes new premiums and "Paid-Up Addition" contributions, and new savings for additional properties. As you repeat the process, your money and your cash flow will compound quickly.

Paid-Up Addition contributions are simply additional cash added to a policy, which then create cash value for about 95 percent of the dollar and an increased death benefit for about 5 percent of the dollar. This enables the cash value to create additional dividends, and the death benefit to protect that cash value and dividend payment from tax. Paid-Up Additions can be paid monthly or annually, but lump sum Paid-Up Additions must be carefully reviewed in order to not create a Modified Endowment Contract. That would cause the whole life insurance policy to have less effective tax law.

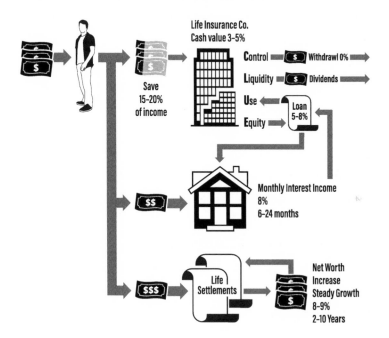

As we've discussed, you should *not* be paying down extra principal on your real estate investment. If you do that, you're tying money up in the walls of your house, essentially turning the property into dead capital. You should instead reinvest that extra money in new properties to increase your cash flow.

THE PITFALLS OF PAYING DOWN
DEBT INSTEAD OF INVESTING

Kim's Client Nearly Loses Everything

One of my clients, a doctor who lived in Florida, invested in five vacation homes on one of the islands off Florida. He had a whole life insurance policy but didn't really believe in its benefits. He paid his premiums, and that was it. He opted instead to sink most of his money into the vacation homes, overhaul them, and heavily prepay the mortgages. I tried to talk him out of it, but to no avail.

Then Hurricane Irene struck and completely wiped out his houses. As a doctor, he had plenty of money, so he decided to repair and rebuild the properties. He had some insurance on the homes, but getting a claim handled takes lots of time and effort. He wanted to get the houses producing cash flow again as soon as possible, so he used his own money instead of waiting for the insurance claims. To finance the repairs, he borrowed against the cash value of his whole life insurance. He borrowed as much as he could, right down to the penny, which is not what I recommend. It's best to leave enough money in the policy for an emergency/opportunity fund. He had $500,000 of cash value in his policy, so I recommended that he borrow only $400,000, leaving $100,000. Instead, he borrowed $475,000.

He did not get the houses rented as quickly as he thought he would, and he called me the next year in distress. The whole situation was a mess. He was worried he would lose his whole life insurance policy, but it had just enough dividends and guaranteed cash value growth that he could borrow against it to pay the monthly premium, which created a little more guaranteed cash value growth, which allowed him to borrow against the policy again. We babysat that policy month by month and every now and then he would have to contribute an additional couple hundred dollars.

Finally, he got the vacation homes rented, and he started slowly paying back the cash-value loan as the monthly rents rolled in. When he got the property and casualty insurance payout, he put it all against his whole life insurance loan as a big lump sum. Finally, over time, he paid off the rest of the loan and got back on his feet. It took close to fifteen years for him to return to where he'd started, and during that time, he had to continue working in his primary role as a doctor.

What is especially amazing about this situation is that the cash value was still growing as an asset. Because of the early years of heavy funding, he'd amassed a large guaranteed cash value of half a million dollars. Since the cash value kept increasing, he was able to borrow against the policy again and continue paying the premium. Every time he paid a premium, the cash value grew again, which allowed him to continue borrowing and paying the premium. In an ideal situation, you would not be borrowing against your policy every month like this, but in his case, it was worth it. In the end, the only money he lost was the interest he paid to the life insurance company along the way, and even that amount was largely offset by the dividend increases and the guaranteed cash value increases.

My client learned a lot of lessons through this experience, and I learned an important one too. This client had just one single large policy, so if he lost it, it would be devastating. I now set up multiple policies, for example $2 million and $3 million, instead of a single $5 million policy in his case. You never want to get rid of a policy, but sometimes life happens, and you're not left with many options. In those cases, having multiple policies gives you flexibility to make adjustments and the ability to jettison one in order to save another.

THE LIE

The lie of this chapter is that paying down principal early is a good thing. In reality, it is much better to reinvest the cash flow you get from a property into your whole life insurance policy and then buy additional properties.

This lie exists because of the myth that all debt is bad when in reality there is good debt and bad debt. When you buy real estate, you're amassing good debt, because the debt is helping you to put money into a house and into your pocket. Paying extra on your principal is risky because you're putting that money into the banker's hands, not your own. When you prepay your mortgage, you lose control of your dollars and get nothing in return except some saved interest. If you believe saving the interest is worth it, you're assuming that you can't beat the interest rate. However, if you put your money *through* a whole life insurance policy instead of paying down your principal early, you can then put that money back to work in another property, and you can easily earn more than the interest rate.

We use the phrase *through* the whole life insurance to help you understand you are paying a premium and possibly a Paid-Up Addition contribution and then you're turning around and borrowing against those dollars for the down payment on your real estate. Alternatively, prepaying your mortgage can put you into a tricky situation in down cycles and liquidity crunches, like what the doctor in Florida experienced. People tend to think they'll be able to access the money they've put into a house if needed, but you won't always be able to refinance or sell a house in order to pull money out. Money that is tied up in a house is dead capital.

Instead of paying down your principal early, you should pay back your whole life insurance policy loan. Then, once you have the capital freed up within your whole life insurance policy, you buy another house. This rinse-and-repeat approach to real estate and whole life insurance is cyclical—more whole life insurance gets you more real estate gets you more whole life insurance and on and on.

WHEN YOU SHOULD *NOT* RINSE AND REPEAT

There are a few strategic exceptions when it doesn't make sense to keep accumulating more cash-flow assets in this rinse-and-repeat approach.

The first such situation is when you experience rapid appreciation on a property. Sometimes certain markets appreciate faster than others, and you can accumulate a lot of extra equity in a house through appreciation. In that case, the extra equity is dead capital. If you sell or refinance the house to pull money out, you can potentially double down and put that money into two separate properties, rebalancing your portfolio to support more cash flow.

The other situation is once you hit your strike number. At that point, the rinse-and-repeat model doesn't matter as much. You may decide to liquidate certain properties to get cash to spend on any variety of things. Remember, though, that you should never sell off so much of your portfolio that you drop below your strike number.

PAYING OFF YOUR PRINCIPAL

If your true goal is to pay off a house early, you will be able to pay it off earlier with the money growing in a whole life insurance policy than paying down the principal. The extra money will grow faster inside your whole life insurance policy than it will in the walls of the house.

This loan analysis calculator from www.TruthConcepts.com illustrates the inefficiency of prepaying a mortgage.

On the left is a thirty-year amortized loan with extra principal payments of $262.18. This amount is the fifteen-year payment of $739.60 minus the thirty-year payment of $477.42 for a difference of $262.18 being applied towards principal on the thirty-year note (instead of choosing a fifteen-year mortgage where the $739.60 payment is required).

On the right is a typical thirty-year amortized loan with no extra principal (or pre-) payments, instead that $262.18 difference is being saved into a whole life insurance policy's Paid Up Addition rider. These typically earn around 4 percent at current writing after fees and without taxes.

Consequently, the strategy on the right has more liquid savings ($64,543) than the left. The calculator below is showing the exact same situation as above at the 180-month (or fifteen-year) mark.

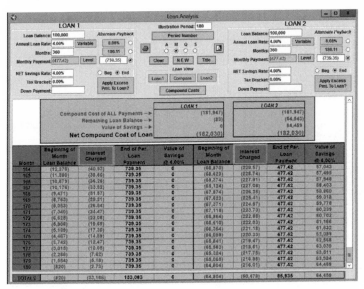

Putting your money into your whole life insurance is also less risky. You could get halfway toward paying off your house, having prepaid the mortgage by an extra $50,000, but if something happens and you're unable to make a monthly payment, you will still go into foreclosure. If you tell a banker to use the money you've prepaid to count toward that month's payment, they'll tell you tough luck. When the money is in your whole life insurance policy, you remain in control of it.

If you pay the principal early, you're lowering the bank's risk while increasing your own. You also lower your cash-on-cash return. All the bank does with the extra principal is re-lend it to another real estate investor. Banks are one of the greatest practitioners of velocity of money. They don't want money sitting around doing nothing. They get it moving by lending it out and earning interest on it.

Banks will tell you to buy a house on a fifteen-year mortgage and prepay it, but that's not what they do. They own real estate themselves, purchased with a thirty-year mortgage, and they certainly don't prepay those mortgages. Banks tell people to lock money into 401(k)s and 529 plans while the banks instead choose to create velocity and movement with their own assets.

Banks also own large amounts of whole life insurance, or BOLI (bank-owned whole life insurance) on their executives and key employees, per the article "Bank Owned Whole life insurance: A Little-Known Way Banks Make Money" written by Matthew Frankel for The Motley Fool[10]. They label their capital in tiers based on quality, and whole life insurance cash value is in the top tier. This is clear evidence that whole life insurance policies are a valid strategy for storing cash. Paying a premium creates the movement of money (velocity) for banks, just like it does for individuals. They do not take their stable tier one capital and invest it in mutual funds.

When it comes to how you handle your money, you should do as the banks do, not as they say. We find this odd that the banks

---

10 https://www.fool.com/investing/general/2015/05/18/bank-owned-life-insurance-a-little-known-way-banks.aspx

practice one thing and preach another. There's a huge hypocrisy in the fact that banks tell you to invest your money in qualified plans while they do the opposite. Banks essentially invest in the same thing we've been talking about this entire book: whole life insurance and real estate. While they are telling you to invest in qualified plans, they are doing the exact opposite.

What we suggest is a way to get money moving (creating velocity) and saving in whole life insurance policies.

Another reason to put extra money into your whole life insurance policy instead of toward your mortgage is to reap the tax benefits. The tax deduction for interest on your primary and secondary home mortgages is one of the few remaining legitimate tax deductions for individuals today. Why would you want to reduce your tax deduction by putting extra money toward your mortgage? Furthermore, the growth of life insurance is tax-deferred. Compare that to where most people store their liquidity: savings accounts and money market funds, both of which are taxed.

Chapter 7

LEVERAGE THE TAX SYSTEM

Anyone may arrange his affairs so that his taxes shall be as low as possible; he is not bound to choose that pattern which best pays the treasury. There is not even a patriotic duty to increase one's taxes.

Over and over again the Courts have said that there is nothing sinister in so arranging affairs as to keep taxes as low as possible. Everyone does it, rich and poor alike and all do right, for nobody owes any public duty to pay more than the law demands.

—Judge Learned Hand, *Helvering v. Gregory*, 69 F.2

Tax destroys both liquidity and velocity of dollars. When you pay high taxes, you have fewer dollars working for you. If, for example, you're operating in an environment that has high income tax, for every dollar you make, you will end up with only sixty cents. If your goal is to maximize long-term returns, the most important thing for you to do is to reduce your tax as much as possible.

You can use whole life insurance policies to get a float on tax dollars. Whole life insurance provides tax-deferred growth, tax-free loans, and income-tax-free death benefits. The combination of tax-beneficial real estate law with tax-beneficial whole life insurance law makes the system put forth in this book incredibly tax efficient. Because real estate involves providing housing for people, the government sees it as benefiting the "greater good" and so has made it a very favorable environment for taxes. While there are caveats, both real estate and whole life insurance are essentially tax-free asset classes. Tax efficiency is crucial, because the highest lifetime expense we all have is taxes.

One of the core philosophies of our cash-flow system is that you shouldn't put money into things that don't give you something in return. Taxation is the epitome of having money taken from you while getting nothing in return. According to Tom Wheelwright with WealthAbility, "What most people don't realize, in fact, is that 99 percent of the Internal Revenue Code is a series of incentives, primarily for businesses and investors to fuel the economy."[11] Real estate investing, along with whole life insurance policies, is the best mitigation for your highest lifetime expense.

---

11 Wheelwright, Tom. Third paragraph in "How Amazon and Entrepreneurs Can Pay Zero Federal Income Tax, and Do So Legally." www.entrepeneur.com. May 15, 2018. Accessed June 8, 2018. https://www.entrepreneur.com/article/313331.

With reduced taxation, we can do more good. We can hire more people, get more properties, and create value far beyond what we can get through paying taxes. Thus, the best investment you can make is reducing your taxes.

THE IMPACT OF REDUCED TAXES ON YOUR STRIKE NUMBER

Jimmy Beats the System

Back when I was still working in medical sales, putting in eighty-hour workweeks, I would come home exhausted and mad and would refuse to talk to anyone. I was attempting to save money to buy real estate at this time, so even though I made a good income, my family wasn't taking vacations or doing anything fun in our nonexistent free time. My wife shopped at a nice suburban grocery store, and one day she purchased a package of brand-name diapers. With three young kids in diapers, this was quite the expense. I saw the bill and told her, "Go buy the cheap stuff!" My wife had had enough. She spun around and said, "Hey, this isn't working. Use your brain and find a different path, one where you're not giving 40 percent of your income to the government."

She was right. Essentially, I was stepping over dollars for pennies and worrying about our grocery bill instead of growing and creating. I didn't have the self-confidence to go create anything on my own. I was in scarcity and trying to cut corners and pennies, thus making our life completely miserable. It was a pure example of a scarcity mindset.

It was time for a change. I compared the money I'd been making as a w-2 employee to the cash flow I would get through investing in real estate. At the time, I made $300,000 in w-2 income but maybe kept $180,000 of it. I had stopped contributing to my 401(k) to add to my monthly cash flow, and that's when I realized I didn't have to reach $300,000 a year. I didn't have to replace my entire w-2 income, I only had to generate $180,000. In reality, to live very comfortably, I only needed $120,000. Because of the tax benefits I would reap as an investor, I didn't need to make as much as I did as a w-2 employee to reach my strike number.

SCARCITY MINDSET

According to Dan Sullivan of Strategic Coach, everyone deals with a scarcity mindset. Even when you change your mindset to one of abundance, you aren't fixed for the rest of your life, you will find yourself falling into a scarcity mindset and panicking. Perhaps even daily. We all go through it. The goal is not *staying* out of it, it's *getting* out of it. Whatever you need to do, do it—go outside, run, pet the dogs, call your best friend, even scream if you need to. In a scarcity mindset, we make poor decisions, especially financial and leadership ones. We are not superhuman, constantly in abundance mindset, so sometimes the fear of being broke keeps us going. The key is recognizing a scarcity mindset and turning it into abundance.

WHAT YOU MAKE VS. WHAT YOU KEEP

Most people think they must replace their entire income in order to gain financial freedom through real estate investment. However, you don't need to replace what you make, only what you *keep*. Due to taxes, there's a big difference between your w-2 income and your strike number. While you might make a hefty salary on your w-2, the government takes a substantial proportion, up to 40 percent for many people.

Take these examples:

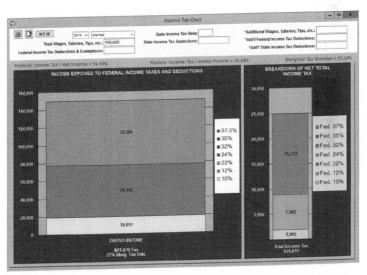

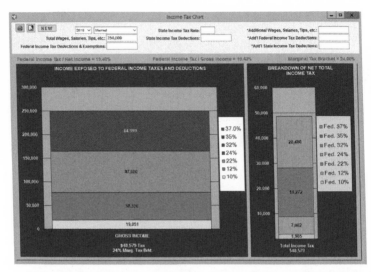

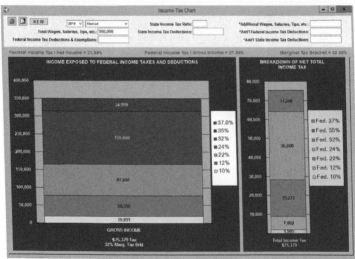

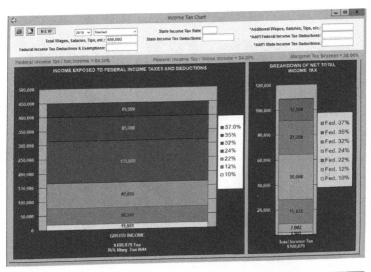

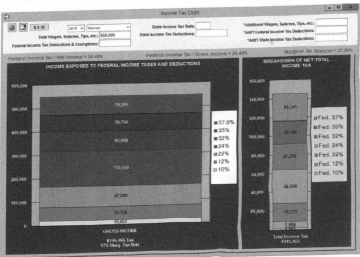

119

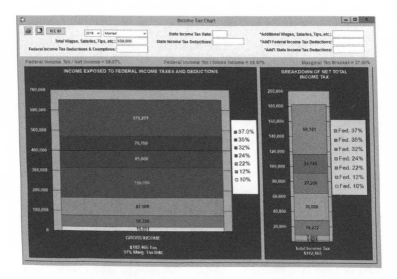

Trying to replace your entire income can seem like an insurmountable goal, but replacing just your after-tax income is much more attainable.

THE LIE

The lie here is that tax (not just debt) is a certainty. When it comes to taxes, most people give up too easily, simply accepting that taxes are a foregone conclusion. They don't understand the types of tax advantages that exist or how easy it is to make use of them. If you simply work at it with a vengeance for a fairly short period of time, you can drastically reduce your taxes.

The only ways to reduce your taxes are to take a lower-paying job, to have no income and thus no taxes, or to own real estate.

The whole life insurance industry, as in books like *The Power of Zero*, puts forth a lie that you can get all of your income from whole life insurance alone, but we adamantly believe that whole life insurance works best in conjunction with real estate. The idea behind this lie is that people can build up large whole life insurance policies and then borrow against the policies for tax-free income. If you borrow against your policy, it *is* tax-free income, but the issue is that some people start these loans as early as sixty years old. If these people live another thirty years, that's thirty years of paying interest on a loan that continually increases as they keep borrowing more and more every year to live on. As they borrow repeatedly, eventually the interest payments can become so high that the policy is no longer able to sustain itself.

It's much more efficient to leave the whole life insurance policy alone and build up real estate investments to create cash flow. When you're eighty-five or ninety and don't want to deal with real estate anymore, you can begin to divest yourself from your portfolio. You can do this by selling properties or using a Charitable Remainder Trust strategy. Before then, though, you should let real estate drive your income, whether it's through bridge loans, lease-to-owns, hard money, or owning turnkey properties. You should save the whole life insurance cash value for your later years and potentially even hold on to it for the death benefit. Doing this is substantially safer, as if you try to live off only your whole life insurance and don't time it right, you could implode your policy.

If you follow the typical financial planning advice you've been fed, you won't be taking advantage of operating in a tax-efficient environment. You will be falling into the myth of the middle class—that going to school, paying your taxes, and funding your qualified retirement plan will allow you to quit working.

While death may be certain, taxes are not. Qualified retirement plans are only forty years old, and income tax has only been around since the late nineteenth century. Americans fought the Revolutionary War over a 6 percent consumption tax, the stamp tax. The income tax was declared unconstitutional twice, and the constitution had to be amended to get the tax passed. There has always been an American aversion to paying income tax, and for 140 years, Americans did not pay income tax at all. Income tax was created by bureaucrats, and those same people came up with qualified retirement plans. They are both new developments of the Industrial Age. They are not certainties. They could be anomalies that go away. In contrast, real estate is a 2,500-year-old industry, and whole life insurance can be traced to 600 BC. According to Encyclopædia Britannica[12], the Greeks and Romans created guilds to which people contributed. When a worker was injured or died, the money was used to care for the family members.

---

12 Greene, Mark Richard. "Insurance." *Encyclopædia Britannica*. October 03, 2018. https://www.britannica.com/topic/insurance/Historical-development-of-insurance.

This is an example of an accumulation mindset vs. a cash flow mindset. The flaw is in thinking you can accumulate fiat dollars somewhere and then draw it down over time. With a cash-flow mindset, you accumulate capital and then put it into assets that continue to kick off cash. You never draw on your seed capital; instead, you let it work over and over for you.

TAXES IN APPRECIATION-BASED REAL ESTATE

The appreciation model of real estate is a high-tax environment. While you can make money buying a house, fixing it up, and then immediately putting it back on the market and selling it—as seen on HGTV shows like *Flip This House*—you will pay at least 35 percent of that money to the government due to the capital gains tax.

When you instead focus on a cash-flow model, you get major tax benefits. You can deduct the interest and get depreciation. You can also do a 1031 exchange, which allows you to sell a property, reinvest the proceeds into a new property, or properties, and defer the capital gains taxes.

Nobody on Wall Street ever talks about their tax liability, their realized gains, or their take-home amount after taxes. They talk only about the top line. The top line sounds glamorous, but at the end of the day, it's the money you *keep*, not the money you make, that truly matters. As such, the cash-flow system is ideal. There are, of course, certain risks involved that you should work to mitigate.

Chapter 8
MITIGATE RISKS

In theory there is no difference between theory and practice; in practice there is.

—Yogi Berra

A s we've spoken about through this book, investing is the act of parting with capital with the expectation of safety of principal and an adequate return on the capital in the form of dividends, interest, or rent. This concept is sourced from *What I Learned Losing a Million Dollars by Jim Paul and Brendan Moynihan.*[13] Investment is something that provides a return with no loss of principal. Typical financial planners

---

13 Paul, Jim and Brendan Moynihan. *What I Learned Losing a Million Dollars.* New York: Columbia Business School Publishing (Columbia University Press). 2013.

frequently talk about *risk tolerance* in relation to investments. They want to quantify it and offer questionnaires to determine possible investments. Many times they lead people to believe that higher risk means the opportunity for bigger returns when in actuality risk only means the likelihood of loss.

The wealthy mitigate and manage risk and actually lower their risk in order to create more wealth. Todd Langford's definition for risk is, "a propensity for loss." People forget this when they take on risk. They feel higher risk automatically equals higher reward, but this is a myth that has been passed on to the masses by Wall Street.

The biggest difference between good investors and great investors is that great investors never lose money. Every single dollar you have working for you is extremely valuable. When you put our system to work, you have the ability for one dollar to grow and compound in several different assets at one time. Each dollar of cash flow you receive contributes either to a down payment on your next house or another dollar toward a new whole life insurance premium, which will kick off more money in the form of either cash flow or whole life insurance dividends, which once again becomes another down payment on real estate or can pay back the loan on the whole life insurance policy. The cycle continues.

Whole life insurance and real estate are both low-risk and antifragile in comparison to other investments. With whole life insurance, you have a guaranteed increase in value every single year, and with real estate, a focus on positive cash flow instead of appreciation can shelter you from losses even if your property value decreases.

When it comes to investing in securities, mutual funds, or qualified plans on Wall Street, there is an absolute risk of ruin. You can lose it all. With whole life insurance, as long as you pay your premiums for a sufficient amount of time, the cash value will never go below a certain mark. With real estate, if you are unable to pay the bank loan, you risk foreclosure or losing the property, but as long as you are compliant with the loan over the thirty-year mortgage, you will always have the brick and mortar of the house. Your risk of going to complete zero is very low.

HIDDEN COSTS

Excel Spreadsheet Millionaires—Jimmy Learns
the Difference between Theory and Practice
One of my first properties was a four-family building in a part of St. Louis called South City. On paper, it looked great. The property cost $85,000, and gross rents were $2,300 a month. When I plugged the numbers into an Excel spreadsheet, I determined the cash flow should be $1,200 a month. I was ecstatic and thought I'd hit the gold mine. With just ten properties like this one, I would be raking in $12,000 of cash flow a month and would have well exceeded my strike number.

An Excel spreadsheet does not reflect reality, though. The map is not the territory, and the spreadsheet didn't account for the fact that the properties in this area were very old, built anywhere between 1900 and 1920. These houses had flat roofs, which almost always have issues, and a lot of deferred maintenance. As a result, the maintenance and repair costs on this building were much higher than on a newer property.

The spreadsheet also failed to consider that this building had two, one-bedroom apartments, which naturally have a higher turnover rate. The people who rent one-bedroom apartments are not people who have families or kids. They're not people who are established and who want to be in that neighborhood for the school district or to settle in a long-term home. With high turnover comes more periods of vacancy.

The final hidden cost omitted from the spreadsheet was all the time I spent chasing rent from bad tenants. Some tenants paid just $450 a month on their units. Anyone who lives in such a low-rent place typically doesn't have a good job and doesn't have their act together overall.

The cash flow had reduced to much less than anticipated and I had to evaluate whether these were the types of properties I wanted to manage. I realized it made more sense to invest in properties that would allow for lease options and tenants that had a much larger sense of ownership in the home.

This was one of my first purchases, and I am still learning lessons and mitigating the risk on it. But real estate is a lot like a bad haircut. I currently have the property leased out to another landlord, and over time, I'll be net cash flow positive. Since that time, I also bought over one hundred additional properties, and so I've spread my risk across all of them, instead of just this one.

SURVIVING A CRASH

Typical financial planning is not investing or saving. It is strictly speculating. In typical investing/speculating strategies, you live or die by appreciation and the underlying value of the asset needs to increase. As a result, you get stuck in a neurotic feedback cycle of constantly checking your account value to see if it's gone up or down that day. When you shift to a cash-flow mindset, you are now able to win in multiple ways. You win when your cash flow comes in every month, you can win if the value appreciates, you win because you are saving taxes, and in many cases, you're using other people's money to make money! Appreciation loses importance because it's only one of the factors. Since you're no longer speculating and only worried about appreciation, if appreciation happens, you're happy. If it doesn't happen, you're still happy because you're winning in three other ways.

Everyone worries about another market crash, yet the value of a cash-flowing real estate portfolio could drop in half tomorrow, and it would not necessarily destroy the investment. As long as the majority of the rents are coming in each month, the cash-flow income will continue to be steady, and the investor will continue to win. This strategy works especially well when an investor purchases the property below market, rehabs the house, and finds a responsible tenant.

Minor fluctuations in rent do occur depending on the market cycle and supply and demand, but the changes in rent are not nearly as dramatic as what can happen to the nominal values of the underlying asset. As long as the cash is flowing, you don't live and die by the undervalue asset of the property, and because you have your cash reserve in your emergency/opportunity fund in the whole life insurance, you will be able to continue to make your mortgage payment and pay for maintenance even without a tenant. This is why the marriage of real estate and whole life insurance works so well. With a thirty-year mortgage and no balloon payment required, your bank won't be making any cash calls, and you'll remain covered during any type of crash.

THE LIE

The lie in this case is that there has to be a lot of risk involved in investing, especially in real estate.

The truth is there is a lot of risk involved in speculating, especially if you don't know what you're doing! Financial planners use computerized evaluations to assign clients a risk-tolerance number. This number is emotional, fluctuates, and is unquantifiable. And as long as the losses don't drop below a certain number, they believe they've done a good job.

Before qualified plans brought every American into the stock market, wealthy people only invested in stocks if they had enough money to move the market. To really win on Wall Street takes a specialization of skills and processes that 95 percent of Americans do not have. There are a select few people who invest in the stock market because they are very good at it, but not every American should be invested and have their nest egg stored on Wall Street, because they have no control. Most people don't have the skillset or mindset to succeed in that game, and there is too much risk. Instead, our system is designed for hard-working, self-educating Americans who are looking to create wealth in alternative, low-risk ways.

With real estate, you have control. You can physically go and see the property, and you can make changes to produce different results. There are still challenges in real estate. Humans are involved, after all, and any time people are involved, challenges are sure to arise. But in general, there's much more stability in cash-flowing real estate than in other investment options. If you want monthly income, real estate is the way to do it. All other forms of monthly income are more volatile. Even bonds, which used to be *the* method to use for safe money, are no longer safe, because municipalities are now going out of business just like businesses do.

Cash-flowing real estate is not volatile, because it is not affected by the things that drive other investments. The stock market doesn't matter. Oil and gas prices don't matter. The president in office doesn't matter. Even higher interest rates don't matter. If interest rates increase, there are less people willing to purchase a property because they do not want to pay those rates. With less buyers available, the purchase price of the property goes down. It's simple supply and demand. When interest rates go down, more people demand houses in the market, thus driving house prices up. When less people are purchasing houses, there are more renters and the price of rents increase.

At the end of the day, everybody needs a house to live in. Shelter is a basic human need. In a down economy, all the luxuries drop by the wayside, but people will continue to do whatever it takes to pay the rent on time. That's why cash-flowing real estate has such low risk. Once you build your portfolio to five to ten properties, your risk drops even further, because if something happens to one property, you still have cash flow from the other houses.

"BLACK SWANS"—THE POTENTIAL RISKS TO WATCH OUT FOR

There are *always* risks, or "black swans," in this or any method of investing, but there are also actions you can take to mitigate those risks. Essentially, you take black swans and make them gray swans by simply acknowledging those risks are out there—and preparing for them.

The first black swan is a tenant not paying rent. The first thing you want to do to reduce this risk is to have a strict rent-collection protocol in place. This way, if a tenant is not paying, you can get them out immediately. Another way to reduce the risk is to use lease options instead of traditional renting. With a lease option, the tenant puts down a nonrefundable option deposit—typically 5 percent of the purchase price—that will go toward their down payment when they purchase the home. Because it's nonrefundable, the tenant now has skin in the game. As a result, you get tenants who have ownership mindsets and who are more likely to pay the rent on time, so that they don't lose their deposit. If the tenant does default and you must evict them, the next person you find will have another option deposit. In that way, you cover some of your vacancy risk.

The next risk is the tenant destroying the property. Using lease options is a great way to mitigate this risk as well. If the tenant destroys the property, you can use the $4,000 nonrefundable deposit to help repair the property. You can also use the option deposit from the next tenant buyer to help offset the vacancy and repair costs.

Another black swan is natural disasters, but the solution to that is simple: buy insurance on everything. Insurance is using someone else's Unique Ability® to cover a risk.

The fourth potential risk is a situation in which you are not collecting rent and so cannot afford to pay the mortgage. This risk is why whole life insurance is so critical. You need a source of liquidity to cover your mortgage payment in case you can't collect rent for any reason. That store of liquidity is your hedge against vacancy. This is a great reason why you should not be paying extra toward your principal and should instead be putting any additional money into your whole life insurance policy for liquidity.

The final major risk is a balloon payment coming due on the property or interest rates skyrocketing. This potential risk is the reason turnkey buyers should always get thirty-year, fixed financing. With fixed financing, you don't have to worry about balloon payments or changing interest rates. A married couple with both partners working can purchase up to twenty houses on a fixed-financing model, and married couples or individuals with a single income can purchase ten. After those limits are reached, the best way to mitigate this risk is to keep a good store of liquidity inside your whole life insurance policy.

You can raise your rents according to inflation while your mortgage payment remains the same. If your money is locked in a qualified retirement plan, inflation will hurt you. You can look at your 401(k) and think, *Wow! I'm going to have a million dollars in thirty years!* In today's dollars, a million dollars is great, but what will the purchasing power of a million dollars be in thirty years? You may only have the purchasing power of $300,000 in today's money. With a thirty-year mortgage, you use inflation on your side. Your mortgage payment will stay the same, but rents will increase approximately 3 percent a year due to inflation. You pay the bank back with inflated dollars thirty years from now that are worth a lot less than they were today.

There are only two things that are benefited by inflation: thirty-year mortgage payments and whole life premiums. This is because both those figures are fixed, and so, while inflation rises, the impact of the payments to the mortgage company and/or to the life insurance company lessens. As in the above mortgage payment example, your $1,000 premium contribution to the life insurance company feels like $300 when you write it thirty years later.

CONCLUSION

Antifragility is beyond resilience or robustness. The resilient resists shocks and stays the same; the antifragile gets better.

—Nassim Nicholas Taleb, *Antifragile: Things That Gain from Disorder*

The whole goal of typical financial planning is to stop trading your time for money, yet very few actually get to the point that they can do that. Financial advisors preach that you need only a percentage of your income to live on, but as Todd Langford has said, "Every day is a Saturday, and you're supposed to spend less?" Not likely! The typical financial approach will never allow people to stop working and find true financial freedom.

The myth of the middle class is that you go to school, get a good job, put money into a qualified plan, and retire at the end of the rainbow in forty years. That model is broken and does not work. In the previous eight chapters, we've laid out a different path—a simple, comprehensive, rinse-and-repeat strategy that is hiding in plain sight. You don't need to make million-dollar grabs, and you don't need to be a fancy economist. You don't have to beat the market, so you don't need an innate ability to pick the best stocks. You also don't need to hire a financial advisor to run through millions and trillions of numbers. Our approach is not new. It has been around for ages, and it's the most powerful, time-tested, antifragile strategy for building wealth.

Once you have your time back, you get to live life, create value, and have fun. The dream here is to get out of the rat race. It's much better to spend the prime years of your life actually living rather than slaving away, waiting until you're sixty-five so you can go on a cruise and sit and stare at the water. After you pay off your whole life insurance loans and get your time back, it's up to you what you do. Real estate investing is your vehicle to get you to the point where you have options. Maybe you're in a job that isn't truly your dream long term. Real estate investing might not be your dream either, but it can allow you to switch to part-time or leave your job entirely so you can pursue other options and figure out what you want to do with your life.

If you want to continue acquiring more assets, go for it! Every time you want to increase your lifestyle, all you have to do is figure out how many more houses you need to buy to support that new strike number.

The beauty of this system is that it will give you true freedom and security, no matter what happens. If you get sick, if you have a car accident—anything at all—you will be protected. This method is unlike anything else in that way. It not only protects against the ups and downs of life; it *overthrows* the ups and downs!

Now, it's up to you. Fulfill your upward potential, make it happen, and find your freedom!

Appendix
WEIGHING YOUR MORTGAGE OPTIONS

Below is an excerpt reprinted with permission from *Busting the Interest Rate Lies written by Kim D. H. Butler with Mona Kuljurgis. Note: Gary is a fictitious client who is in his mid-thirties at this point and has been meeting off and on with his Financial Advisor Emily. We pick them up at a meeting where they discussed which was more efficient, a fifteen- or a thirty-year mortgage.*

Several years passed and Gary continued to do well at his job. His first meeting with Emily Peterson had paid off, and Gary kept his credit cards low and his emergency fund high—and his slightly used car was still looking good and going strong.

But life reared its head, as Emily said it would. Gary's mother and sister had needs their modest incomes couldn't always cover. There were medical bills and car repairs and the house Gary grew up in certainly wasn't new. It always needed a pipe fixed or an appliance replaced, and that hit everyone's budget hard.

By now Gary was renting a nice but small $500 per month apartment near his family. Try as he may to save up for a down payment to buy a house, something with more urgency and greater priority always took place.

But then the greatest and most urgent priority that Gary had known so far came to pass. Gary's aunt, the woman who helped raise him and who'd always treated him like her own son, became ill.

Gary's mother was devastated. She spent every spare waking moment with her sister, driving her to the hospital and various treatments, but Gary's mom had to work as well. Gary joined his mother and his own sister in caring for his aunt, but things had not slowed down at work. Gary had become a full-fledged superintendent, and he now ran entire construction projects on his own. Workdays were long and tiring, and there was little time for days off.

In fact, despite Gary using every last bit of his paid leave during his aunt's illness in a matter of months, he was still left wondering why, at the end of a person's life, they couldn't have their family relaxed, present, attentive, and available around them—instead of haggard, frazzled, and distracted. It all seemed for nothing, he thought, if you couldn't be there for the people you loved when it counted most.

When Gary's aunt succumbed to her illness, he took two weeks of unpaid leave to be there for his very shaken mother, his sister, and to wrap his own head around this new normal. They were a small family, but they were close. And now, they were one fewer.

A couple weeks later, Gary's mother was cleaning out her sister's things and came across a document. It was a whole life insurance policy. The beneficiary listed on the policy was her own son. Unbeknownst to anyone, Gary's aunt had kept up with the policy her entire life. Gary was the beneficiary of a $100,000 benefit.

As Gary and his mom stood in the kitchen looking at the check, they both had an eerie sense of *déjà vu*.

"Well, it seems as though we've been here before, son, though under better circumstances." Gary's mother wiped her eyes. "This is an even bigger check than the last time we stood here." She laughed through recently shed tears.

"Yeah," said Gary. "And I still don't know what to do with it." Gary's heart ached for his mother and his beloved aunt, but he was still serious about his statement.

They both stood quiet for a while, feeling the strange irony of it all.

Then, after a long silence, Gary's mom said, "Your house, honey. Your house. This is money for your house. You've taken care of ours for so long. Now it's time for you to have your own." Then after a long pause, she went on, "Your aunt would have wanted it. Your aunt would have wanted it."

It was true. His aunt would have wanted it. She even spoke of it. She would cut out little listings in the paper and give them to him, she was an open-house addict and stopped at every one she passed. She was on the lists of 12 realtors. In many ways, it was plainly obvious.

"Before you do, though," his mom went on, "why don't you see that woman again, that Financial Advisor. She seemed to do well by you last time. This would seem another good time to pay her a visit."

"I will, Mom. I will." Gary put his hand on his mom's shoulder. They looked at each other and all that passed in the last 30-odd years flashed before them.

* * *

"I'm so sorry to hear about your aunt, Gary." Emily Peterson spoke quietly as she sat across the large wooden desk from him.

"Thank you, Emily. She was a really sweet person. I was lucky to have known her for all this time."

"I have no doubt. And you had no idea about the whole life insurance policy?"

"None at all. Not until my mother found the papers. I wonder why she never said anything."

"Wow. That's a mystery. It's quite a bit of money. The last time you were here we were only talking about a fraction of that amount."

"This is true. Yes, $100,000 is much more. But, Emily, I think I know what I want to do with it. I want to buy a house. I want to buy it outright, to pay cash."

"Wow, Gary. Congratulations. That's exciting news. And paying cash is a gutsy move; it's the right move for many people. Still, I'm a Prosperity Economics Advisor and my mission is to tell the whole truth about your money. So would it be okay if I showed you a few things?"

"Yes, Emily," Gary answered, "of course. That's why I'm here."

"All righty. Good. So, just so you know, home ownership is a different creature than renting. No landlord will pay for repairs or for ongoing maintenance to your place. On account of this, money needs to be set aside for those things...because that water heater will go out and the refrigerator will need to be replaced."

"Oh, you don't have to tell me. I've been dealing with my mother's house for years."

"Okay. Well, then you also know there are taxes due every year on your property, and home owner's insurance."

"Yes, I do. I know that very well—all of that on top of the mortgage payment.

"And that's why I want to pay cash," Gary went on, "then I don't have to think about at least that monthly payment. Plus, paying for the house in cash will save me tens of thousands of dollars in interest, won't it?"

"It may save you an interest payment, but it won't save you an interest cost," replied Emily. "In fact, let's go to the calculators right now."

Emily opened her Truth Concepts software and brought up a Loan Analysis calculator. "Let's see how much interest you'd save by paying cash versus, let's say, taking out a 15-year mortgage."

Emily entered the inputs for the loan's terms:

- $100,000 loan balance
- fifteen-year (180-month) term
- 5% interest rate.

Emily turned her computer screen towards Gary and showed him the calculator in Figure 10.

"As you can see, taking no mortgage would save you $42,343 in interest versus taking out a 15-year mortgage."

Wow, thought Gary, *$42,343—that's a lot of money*. He was dumbfounded, but he was also impressed with his financial savvy for deciding to buy his house outright.

"In fact, while we're at it," said Emily, "let's run the numbers for a 30-year mortgage."

Gary leaned in as Emily changed the loan timeframe in the Loan Analysis calculator:

- $100,000 loan balance
- thirty-year (360-month) term
- 5% interest rate

Up popped the table in Figure 11. Gary was aghast.

"I'm not sure I even believe this," said Gary. "I would pay $93,256 in interest for taking out a $100,000 mortgage over 30 years? That's almost double the cost of the house!"

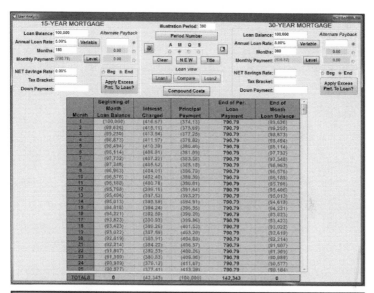

"Yup," said Emily. "That's what the bank charges you for borrowing their $100,000. It's the mechanics of compound

145

interest. It's important to understand those mechanics before you purchase any big-ticket item—and the biggest item most anyone will purchase in their lifetime is a house.

"You'll pay almost double for that house, Gary—close to $200,000—if you take out a loan for 30 years."

Wow, thought Gary again. He couldn't quite believe his ears. $93,256.00 for the privilege of purchasing a home over time? *No way,* he thought, feeling a little bit nauseous. *No way am I paying the bank that kind of money. Thank God, but mostly thank Aunt Emma, for the $100,000 to put down in cash.*

"Well, that settles it," he said. "I'm buying my house for cash. Thank you so much, Emily, for clarifying my options and running those scenarios for me. I'm so glad I came in to see you."

"I'm glad you came in to see me too, Gary. It was really nice seeing you again. But, just before you go, would you mind if I run another calculation or two for you?"

"Um, okay," said Gary. I'm not sure what more there is to be said, he thought, but okay.

"The trick with comparing mortgages," she started, "is to look at the value of the money over time. While it appears that a 15-year mortgage costs less than a 30-year mortgage from the calculations we just did, and cash appears to cost the least, the reality is that you only pay less in interest."

"But besides the principle," Gary interjected, "which was $100,000 in both mortgages we looked at, what else is there to pay besides interest?"

"Opportunity cost," Emily answered. "In other words, by putting your money into a mortgage, what opportunity are you giving up elsewhere? Now, true opportunity cost, in classic economics, looks at the next-best potential use of the money or resource. However, that could be many things—you could put your $100,000 into buying ten cars or collectible art or starting a company or the stock market. It's somewhat subjective. But more importantly, it's impractical to compare every possible use of your money to try to determine what's the 'next-best use.' You follow me?"

"Definitely."

"Okay. So, for our purposes, which is primarily to illustrate the value of the money itself over time—apart from what you could use it for—it makes the most sense to see what that money could grow to if put into a fairly predictable and safe place. Then, we can truly compare dollars to dollars and determine what your mortgage options actually cost you when taking into account the loss of use of that money."

She looked at Gary to make sure he was still on track, and he nodded. Emily turned her computer monitor a little more towards Gary so it was easier for him to see.

"This is a Future Value calculator," she said. "It's simply a compound-interest calculator, which calculates the interest earned on money placed in an interest-bearing account. In other words, it'll show you the future value of your money. Does that make sense?"

"Yep."

"Good. Do you remember, back in the day, when I talked to your high school class about the mechanics of compound interest?"

"I remember that we should earn interest, not owe it." Gary sing-songed the last five words.

"Yes, that's right. Wow, so I guess that stuck, huh? Good! So, when you take out a mortgage, those mechanics are working in the bank's favor. But when you deposit money in an interest-bearing account, it's like you are loaning the bank your money. And you get paid for that. Get it?"

"I do."

"Perfect. So let's take a look at the $100,000 your aunt left you, and let's say you put it into an interest-bearing account paying 5 percent. This could be any type of bank account, a certificate of deposit, money market, or cash value whole life insurance. With me so far?"

"Yes, I am."

"Okay. So, let's see what that adds up to."

Emily entered the inputs and pointed to the table in Figure 12.

The number in the bottom Future Value field was $446,774. "Gary, $100,000 invested at 5 percent over 30 years grows to $446,774—over four times what you put into it."

"Wow!" Gary said. "$446,774...seriously?"

"Yep," Emily answered. "Nearly half a million dollars. And this is what we're assigning as the opportunity cost associated with your getting a mortgage—what you could have earned with that hundred grand if you did not put it into a house."

Present Value: 100,000	**Title**	**Clear**	N E W	
Monthly Payment: 0	• **Beg**	• **End**		
Annual IRate: 5.00%	**A M Q S**		TO P	
Months: 360.00	○ • ○ ○			
Future Value: 446,774				

"That almost makes me want to live in a van instead of buying a house."

"Well, Gary, I'm gonna go out on a limb and say you probably wouldn't want to for 30 years."

"Good point."

"But here's the thing," Emily continued. "We want to compare this with your mortgage costs because, remember, we're trying to see which mortgage—or no mortgage by paying all cash—costs the least. So, to do this, we go back to the Loan Analysis calculator. But this go-around, we factor in the 5 percent Net Savings Rate that we didn't before. This takes into account that the money going into this mortgage is not being put into 5-percent interest-bearing savings."

"Because every payment going toward the mortgage is money I could have put into earning interest?"

"Exactly," she said. "You are denying yourself the opportunity—this is, again, opportunity cost—the ability to earn interest on that money."

"Okay. Got it. And my mortgage interest paid and savings interest earned, the two rates, those are set at 5 percent so we have an equal comparison…is that right?"

"Yes. Good catch. With any financial comparison, you must only change one variable at a time; otherwise, you're comparing apples to oranges. We're looking at the cost of your mortgages, 15 versus 30 years, so every other factor needs to be the same."

"All right," Gary said with a nod. "Let's see how this looks." Emily pulled up the result, shown in Figure 13.

"There you go. Believe it or not, both the 15-year and 30-year mortgages have the same exact compound cost—$446,774. 'Compound cost' is just the term we use for factoring in the time value of the money."

"And," Gary said, "when we came up with the same number in the Future Value Calculator, how does that tie in?"

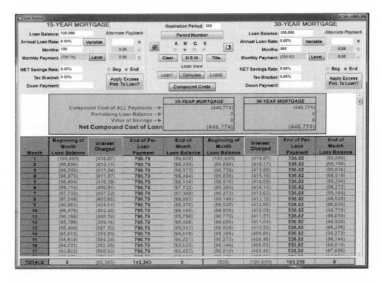

"That would still be, in a sense, your compound cost if you paid $100,000 cash for the house. Think of that scenario as loaning yourself the money, like you are both the mortgage company and the borrower. You loaned yourself the $100,000 by effectively taking it away from being put into your own savings, and thus you 'paid' 5 percent in annual interest because it was 5 percent you could not earn on the money each year."

"Oh, I see. Wow...so whether I pay cash, take a 15-year mortgage, or take a 30-year mortgage, the use of that money is costing me the same over time."

"Yep. Again, you'll pay less in interest on the 15-year mortgage, but overall—when factoring in the time value of money—all three financing scenarios end up costing the same."

"Okay. But then, with everything being equal, why not just pay cash, and then I don't have any mortgage payment to worry about?"

"There's no doubt that most people would feel a huge peace of mind in having no mortgage payment. And peace of mind is worth something. But my job is to show you the economics of your choices. You'll have to ultimately decide on the emotional aspect, your comfort level, but it's important to at least first understand the totality of the situation so you can make the best choice for you. When you have all the information, you can feel assured that you've made your decision with complete understanding."

Gary nodded, and Emily reached into a tray on her desk and pulled out a sheet of paper.

"Gary, being a Prosperity Economics Advisor, I'm guided by seven Principles of Prosperity. Read out loud the fifth principle for me." Emily handed him the Principles of Prosperity handout:

Summary of the 7 Principles of Prosperity™

Think: Owning a Prosperity mindset eliminates Poverty; scarcity thinking keeps you stuck.

See: Increase your Prosperity by adopting a macro-economic point of view—a perspective in which you can see how each one of your economic decisions affects all the others. Avoid microeconomic "tunnel vision."

Measure: Awareness and measurement of opportunity costs enables you to recover them. Ignore this at your peril.

Flow: The true measure of Prosperity is cash flow. Don't focus on net worth alone.

Control: Those with the gold make the rules; stay in control of your money rather than relinquishing control to others.

Move: The velocity of money is the movement of dollars through assets. Movement accelerates Prosperity; accumulation slows it down. Avoid accumulation.

Multiply: Prosperity comes readily when your money "multiplies"—meaning that one dollar does many jobs. Your money is disabled when each dollar performs only one or two jobs.

Source: *Busting the Financial Planning Lies: Learn to Use Prosperity Economics to Build Sustainable Wealth*. Copyright © 2012 Prosperity Economics Movement, www.ProsperityPeaks.com.

Gary read: *Control—Those with the gold make the rules; stay in control of your money rather than relinquishing control to others.*

"Yes," Emily said. "Maintaining control and decision-making power over your money is a key principle. When you hand $100,000 in cash over to buy a property, your control over that money disappears."

Emily paused for a moment, then became very serious.

"But there's something far more important, Gary," she said quietly.

"Remember telling me how much you wished you could be there for your aunt as she became ill? Remember telling me how much you cared for her, how she helped raise you as a child and had been there for you your entire life, through thick and thin?"

Gary nodded and dropped his eyes to the floor.

"Remember telling me how sick it made you to watch her suffer, knowing you couldn't walk away from your job and regular paycheck, and that you'd used up all your time off?"

Gary choked back some emotion. He was silent.

Emily continued on quietly, "Well, imagine if at that time you'd had some money to fall back on. Imagine if there had been money in the bank to simply say to your boss, 'My aunt is ill. She helped raise me, and she needs me now. I'm going to be there for her.'

"You could have also said, 'I hope my job is here when I return. But if not, then that's okay. My family is my priority now. And I'm not going to confuse my priorities.'"

Gary remained silent and still. He could not meet Emily's eyes. "I'm not saying this to rub salt into your wounds, Gary. I'm saying it because, regardless of the amount that money grows to in 30 years, having a cash reserve at every stage in life is imperative—cash that is available, accessible, and ready to use when life hits you, broadside, just as it did you and your aunt this past year."

Gary finally looked up.

"And though I don't want to be morose, Gary, life can be completely upended in a minute."

Gary looked wide-eyed.

"But it's not only the most drastic of circumstances we're considering here. Let's work with something not so dire. What if the roof on that house of yours needs replacing in 15 years? Or the water heater? Or you told me you're planning on getting married soon. What if you could pay for that wedding in cash?"

Emily watched Gary thoughtfully.

"Imagine being debt free after the wedding? Or after making improvements on your property? Having the cash around to address those situations can be the difference between serious stress and overwhelm and a feeling of peace and calm.

"You're still young, Gary. Get some miles on you and you'll realize having a cash reserve can be pivotal, in the good times and the bad, throughout every stage in your life."

Gary listened quietly.

"So," Emily continued, "just for argument's sake, let's say you couldn't keep your savings untouched for 30 years, and you needed to tap that money in half the time. Let's see what that $100,000 would grow to if you stuck it in an account for 15 years."

Emily entered some inputs and brought up the Future Value chart in Figure 14.

"After 15 years, you'd have $211,370. How much time could that buy you, Gary, if you had to go through it all again with your mother, your sister, or a friend?"

"A lot of time," Gary replied, "$211,370 would buy me a lot of time," and then more lightly, "and in the best-case scenario, a lot of new roofs and water heaters."

Emily smiled, "Yes. A lot of new roofs and water heaters."

Gary sat quietly for a while, considering his potential cash reserve. Then, Emily's thoughts seemed to shift.

"One more thing, Gary. Know this. Success is discipline. These methods, the methods of Prosperity Economics, are not for the faint of heart. They're not for everyone."

"Oh?" replied Gary.

"No. Having an accessible and available $100,000 laying around, compounding into even more money every year, can be tempting—tempting enough to blow on exotic vacations or a man cave in your new home."

"True."

"So, if you feel you're the type of person who will access that money indiscriminately or without regard, then this strategy is not for you. In that case, you should absolutely buy your house for cash. You can always take what would have been your mortgage payment and stick it into an interest-bearing account each month. In fact, if you do that and earn 5 percent each year, you'll wind up with the same $211,370 after 15 years and $446,774 after 30 years—if you can maintain the resolve not to touch it."

"Ummm."

"And there's no judgment in that, at all, Gary. Knowing yourself is a wise and responsible way to go through life. Alternately, making minimum credit card payments or trying to impress friends with your dear aunt's bequest is not."

"Well, that's definitely not me."

"I'm confident of that, Gary. You know that I'm mostly making a point. Keeping the money in your control, following that Principle of Prosperity Economics, puts that money there to catch you when you fall—or someone you love. It's for that or for helping you reach financial independence. Either one. But it's not to tap into when you are tempted to overspend one month or to make up for the habit of overspending."

Gary listened soberly. Emily's tone was serious and a bit severe, but it didn't throw him. Gary had known people who had received generous gifts, large bonus checks, and other substantial lump sums and blown them in a year, ending up with nothing to show. He wasn't fazed by Emily's sternness.

They sat in silence for a moment. Then Gary whispered, "Big hat. No cattle."

"What...?" said Emily.

Gary chimed again, "Big hat. No cattle. My grandfather used to say it. It refers to people who prance around in fancy things but ultimately don't have a pot to...well, you know... don't have a chamber pot."

"Yes, I do know," laughed Emily. "I'm a Financial Advisor. I do know. It's important to own a chamber pot, Gary, long before you own fancy things. It's important to have ground under your feet, a roof over your head, and a savings to fall back on—and to make that your first priority."

"Mmmm."

"But that's not to say you shouldn't enjoy your windfall, Gary. Take 10 percent right now and go out and spend it on something you love. Maybe go on a fancy honeymoon after the wedding, or furnish that house of yours. It's not all gloom and doom. You should be able to enjoy some of your money at the time you receive it."

"That would be great, Emily. I would really like that."

"Excellent."

"Wow," he said. "I really got more than I bargained for on this visit! I wasn't counting on all this information and the new perspective."

"Good, Gary. That new perspective is what I'm counting on, so I'm glad you came to it. It's why I do this. But you're not getting off that easy. I've got one more calculation to show you."

"What?"

"Yes. Let's run through one more scenario."

"Okay, okay, fine." He smiled at his feigned exasperation.

"With all the talk of compounding interest, we haven't talked about the mortgage interest tax deduction the government hands out as an incentive for taking out a mortgage."

"What?"

"Yep, it's true. So let's do that."

Emily pulled up the Loan Analysis calculator they'd been working on and entered the inputs for a $100,000 loan at 5 percent over 30 years. Gary saw that Emily entered values into two fields that until now had remained blank: the Tax Bracket field and the NET Savings Rate field. She pointed to the chart in Figure 15A.

"Okay, Gary. In column four, titled End of Period Loan Payment, we see the monthly payment of your 30-year mortgage — $536.82."

"Yep, I see that," said Gary.

"Good. Now to the left of that, the second column, titled Interest Charged, is the proportion of that monthly payment going to interest every month.

"Even though your payment stays the same each month at $536.82, the proportion of it going to interest decreases just a little every month as the proportion of it going to principle increases by the same amount. With me so far?"

"Yes," Gary replied.

"Excellent. The reason for this, as column one labeled Beginning of Month Loan Balance shows you, is that your total loan balance, the entirety of the mortgage, decreases each month with every mortgage payment."

"Oh, I see." answered Gary.

"Yes. Not so hard, huh? Now, let's look at something new. This is different.

"The far-right column, titled Value of Savings @5%, is a new calculation.

"The reasoning behind it goes like this: Because the government wants to encourage home ownership, and because they know most people cannot afford to pay cash to buy their homes outright, the government allows you to deduct your mortgage interest from your taxes.

"That means that the interest you pay on your mortgage each year can be subtracted from your taxable income—whatever it amounts to won't be taxed."

"Um, okay," replied Gary, looking confused and unimpressed.

"So. Let's put it this way. You're in the 25 percent tax bracket, correct? After all your exemptions and deductions are tallied, the top level of your income will be taxed at 25 percent."

"Yes, that's correct," replied Gary.

"So that last column is just that. It's 25 percent of the mortgage interest displayed in column two. The first value in the far-right column is $104. That's 25 percent of the first value in the second column, $416.67. For your income level, this is what you would save in taxes for that month."

"Okay. I see that," responded Gary.

"Excellent. So this is where it gets a bit confusing. The far-right column is not just a straight 25 percent of the interest shown in column two—it is the cumulative sum of that interest each month, increasing by a factor of 5 percent."

"Um," muttered Gary.

"For instance, let's take month number seven. The interest due that month is $413.63, and 25 percent of that equals $103.

Added to the value of the previous month six, $630, that only equals $733. The reason month seven is three dollars more, $736, is because of the 5 percent interest that's been compounding since the beginning."

"Oh, okay, I get it," said Gary.

"Yeah. So there are a couple calculations going on over there. Keep that in mind."

"Okay," said Gary.

"So, Gary, take a look at month 12, in the Value of Savings column. What is the amount there?"

"$1,271."

"Correct. Excellent. That's your tax savings that first year."

Gary looked confused and then asked, "So this all means I'll have to calculate my anticipated mortgage interest tax deduction, pull it out of my salary, and invest it every month?"

"Well, no," answered Emily, "the deduction happens automatically when you file your taxes—you report the interest you pay, which causes the deduction, and your income on the same tax form. If you'd paid cash, you wouldn't get the deduction. So treat the deduction as a bonus. Save it and leave your emergency account alone."

"Okay. Well, how much money could I earn?"

"As we saw, $1,271 for the first year, to start. But let's extrapolate that out to the end of the loan, to month 360 at the bottom of that far-right column. Do you know what you would have?"

"Nope."

"After investing your mortgage interest tax savings for 30 years at 5 percent, you'd have $63,580." She showed him the screen in Figure 15B.

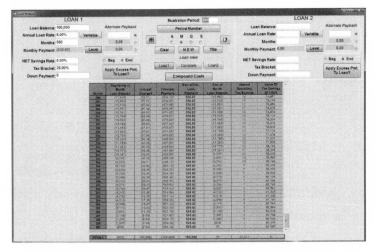

Gary was again silent. He couldn't believe all this money could result from simply putting his inheritance into a savings, investment, or cash value whole life insurance account—and pulling his mortgage payment from his paycheck.

"And by the way," Emily continued, "what I just showed you is another reason why 15-year mortgages are not better than 30-year ones. Because you pay less in interest on a 15-year mortgage, that means you also get less of a tax deduction. So, when you factor in the time value of saving that tax deduction on a 15-year mortgage, you actually come out worse off than doing the same with a 30-year mortgage. You also won't have that $63,580 tax benefit if you pay cash for the house, either!" (See Figure 16.)

	15-YEAR MORTGAGE							30-YEAR MORTGAGE	
Loan Balance: 100,000		Alternate Payback		Illustration Period: 186			Loan Balance: 100,000		Alternate Payback
Annual Loan Rate: 5.00%	Variable			Period Number		Annual Loan Rate: 5.00%	Variable		
Months: 180		0.00		A M Q S		Months: 360		0.00	
Monthly Payment: (790.79)	Level	0.00		Clear NEW Title		Monthly Payment: (536.82)	Level	0.00	
NET Savings Rate: 5.00%	Beg End			Loan View		NET Savings Rate: 5.00%		Beg End	
Tax Bracket: 25.00%	Apply Excess		Loan1 Compare Loan2		Tax Bracket: 25.00%		Apply Excess	
Down Payment: 0	Pmt. To Loan?			Compound Costs		Down Payment: 0		Pmt. To Loan?	

	15-YEAR MORTGAGE	30-YEAR MORTGAGE
Compound Cost of ALL Payments →	(211,370)	(143,486)
Remaining Loan Balance →	0	(67,864)
Value of Savings →	17,405	24,490
Net Compound Cost of Loan	(193,966)	(186,860)

Month	Beginning of Month Loan Balance	Interest Charged	End of Per. Loan Payment	Value of Savings @ 5.00%	Beginning of Month Loan Balance	Interest Charged	End of Per. Loan Payment	Value of Savings @ 5.00%
1	(100,000)	(416.67)	790.79	104	(100,000)	(416.67)	536.82	104
2	(99,626)	(415.11)	790.79	208	(99,880)	(416.17)	536.82	209
3	(99,250)	(413.54)	790.79	313	(99,759)	(415.66)	536.82	313
4	(98,873)	(411.97)	790.79	417	(99,638)	(415.16)	536.82	419
5	(98,494)	(410.30)	790.79	521	(99,516)	(414.65)	536.82	524
6	(98,114)	(408.81)	790.79	626	(99,394)	(414.14)	536.82	630
7	(97,732)	(407.22)	790.79	730	(99,272)	(413.63)	536.82	736
8	(97,348)	(405.62)	790.79	834	(99,148)	(413.12)	536.82	842
9	(96,963)	(404.01)	790.79	939	(99,025)	(412.60)	536.82	949
10	(96,576)	(402.40)	790.79	1,043	(98,900)	(412.09)	536.82	1,056
11	(96,188)	(400.78)	790.79	1,148	(98,776)	(411.57)	536.82	1,163
12	(95,798)	(399.16)	790.79	1,253	(98,650)	(411.04)	536.82	1,271
13	(95,406)	(397.53)	790.79	1,357	(98,525)	(410.52)	536.82	1,378
14	(95,013)	(395.89)	790.79	1,462	(98,398)	(409.99)	536.82	1,487
15	(94,618)	(394.24)	790.79	1,566	(98,272)	(409.46)	536.82	1,595
16	(94,221)	(392.59)	790.79	1,671	(98,144)	(408.93)	536.82	1,704
17	(93,823)	(390.93)	790.79	1,776	(98,016)	(408.40)	536.82	1,813
TOTALS	(786)	(42,343)	142,343	17,405	(68,137)	(32,116)	96,628	24,490

"Interesting," Gary said. "That makes sense."

"Now remember, all of this will require you to make that mortgage payment from your salary, and not simply let that money flow into your general expenses, as would likely be your choice if you paid cash. I hope you understand the point, now that you have seen what kind of return it would get you."

Gary nodded.

"Most importantly, though, as your aunt's inheritance grows over your lifetime, you will have access to it. It's money that is there in case you lose your job, if another family member becomes sick, or that house of yours needs major repair. It's there for you to fall back on. Remember, that's the 'Control' aspect we talked about earlier."

Gary remained silent. After a moment, he asked:

"But all my friends say I should put down as much as I can on the house. They're all saving up diligently for their own down payments, trying to save as much as they can before taking out a mortgage."

"Great that they're saving, but not great that they'll put that money into the house. Remember how we saw that the cost of the house over time is the same whether you pay cash, take out a 15-year mortgage, or take out a 30-year mortgage? Well, the same thing applies whether you pay all cash or part in cash—in other words, a down payment. So, this brings us back again to control of your money. Whatever you put down, whether it's 10 percent or 20 percent or whatever, you've lost control of that money."

"But it's equity, right? I mean, I can take out a home-equity loan if I needed to, right?"

"True. But the thing is, you have to apply for it and qualify for it, it goes on your credit, and worst of all, you end up paying interest to the bank to use that money! Actually, the worst of it is that your house is on the line—if something bad happens and you default on that home-equity loan, you could lose your home." Gary let that sink in before Emily continued.

"Conversely, if you keep the money out of the house and in a savings-type account, you can either access it at no cost or borrow against it with far less risk. In cash value whole life insurance, for example, if you couldn't pay that loan back—ever, in your entire life—nothing would happen to your credit, you wouldn't lose your home, and the repayment would just come out of your death benefit."

"Wow," he said. "So, minimum down is really the way to go?"

"Yep," she said. "Keep control of your money. Everything you put into the house is at risk until you own it outright. You could make 300 payments perfectly on time, 25 years into your mortgage, and if something happens that causes you to default on your payments, you could lose all that money you paid and your house. Conversely, your money kept outside of the house, building up in a reliable interest-bearing account, that's your safety net in the event anything happens."

"All right, Emily. You've sold me. Minimum down on the house, and I'll save and invest my aunt's money."

"Perfect. You have an amazing opportunity here. You have the chance to buy the house and maintain a growing cash reserve over your lifetime. Many people don't have this opportunity—and many, if they have it, don't take advantage of it."

Gary nodded in complete agreement.

"There are rainy days to come, Gary, and there are bright and sunny ones. Keeping well-tended cash on hand not only helps you cushion life's blows—it also helps take advantage of life's opportunities when they come around." Emily reached into her file, took out a publication entitled *A Home-Buyer's Guide* and handed it to Gary. "Happy house hunting," she said with a smile.

THE PROSPERITY
ECONOMICS MOVEMENT

Before the rise of today's financial planning industry, and its focus on market-based retirement planning, people built wealth over time with diligence, common sense, and a long-term view. Instead of creating ever-changing stock portfolios and restrictive 401(k) plans, investors built equity through property ownership, business development, and dividend-paying whole life insurance. "Financial planning" as we know it today was the exception, not the rule.

Here's the thing: most wealthy people today still build their wealth exactly the same way, using principles we like to call "Prosperity Economics." It's usually only the rest of us—busy, uninformed, confused, and new to investing—that don't follow these time-tested practices for building real wealth.

Why? Partially because we don't know any better, but mostly, because we're never taught Prosperity Economics. Instead, we are steered away from proven, traditional methods of creating wealth, and directed to become buyers of a puzzling maze of complicated financial instruments and vehicles that don't even make sense to the people who sell them. Mutual funds have become so intricate that even explaining how they work is practically impossible, let alone predicting when they'll make or lose money. And as if that weren't bad enough, over 30 percent of the average investor's hard-earned money gets siphoned off in administration and management fees—paid to Financial Advisors who often have conflicts of interest.

Prosperity Economics reintroduces traditional and trusted ways to grow and protect your money reliably and sustainably. Prosperity Economics is an alternative to "typical" financial planning that shows you how to control your own wealth instead of trusting your financial security and growth to conflicted corporations, complex government oversight, and fickle market forces.

Now, typical financial planning is better than nothing. But we believe that you, no matter how much or little you know about investing or money management, can do a lot better. This is why we created the Prosperity Economics Movement. This movement is actually comprised of smaller movements that represent alternatives to a financial planning industry we believe has gone off course. You may have heard of the Infinite Banking Concept, Private or Family Banking, Rich Dad Strategies, Circle of Wealth, or Bank on Yourself. Advisors and agents within the movement may use different language and even suggest different financial strategies, but they honor a common set of principles, such as the 7 Principles of Prosperity™ articulated by Kim Butler.

The Prosperity Economics Movement (PEM) has two websites, ProsperityPeaks.com for American investors and consumers, and ProsperityEconomicsAdvisors.com for advisors and other financial professionals. Prosperity Peaks helps people like you discover how you can take back control of your thinking and your finances. Prosperity Economics Advisors is a community that helps insurance advisors develop a prosperity mindset and learn the best ways to help their clients achieve long-term financial success.

IMPLEMENTING PROSPERITY ECONOMICS

With Prosperity Economics, wealth isn't measured by how much money you have, but by how much freedom you have with your money. We focus on reliable, real-time cash flow rather than a far-off net worth number that you can never use to improve your life.

Our priorities are liquidity, control, and safety, not gambling on a high rate of return you may never see. Prosperity Economics gives you the flexibility to live your unique life to the fullest, along with the reliable cash flow to support whatever kind of life you choose yours to be—in other words, to reach your financial peaks.

ADDITIONAL RESOURCES

RECOMMENDED READING

5 Day Weekend by Nik Halik and Garrett B. Gunderson. Published by Bard Press.

Busting the Interest Rate Lies by Kim D. H. Butler. Published by Prosperity Economics Movement.

Busting the Retirement Lies by Kim D. H. Butler. Published by Prosperity Economics Movement.

Live Your Life Insurance by Kim D. H. Butler. Published by CreateSpace Independent Publishing Platform.

The Mystery of Capital by Hernando De Soto. Published by Basic Books.

Rich Dad Poor Dad by Robert T. Kiyosaki. Published by Plata Publishing.

The Sovereign Individual by James Dale Davidson and William Rees-Mogg. Published by Touchstone.

WEBSITES

TruthConcepts.com

BustingTheRealEstateInvestingLies.com

REAL ESTATE CALCULATOR

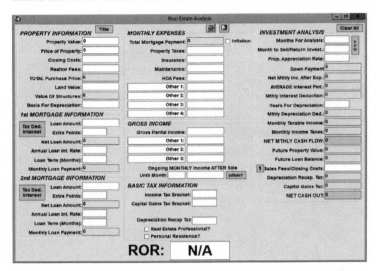

This real estate calculator from www.TruthConcepts.com helps us gather the information necessary to analyze an Investment Real Estate Deal.

This blog post explains the calculator: http://truthconcepts.com/how-do-i-tell-if-my-real-estate-deal-is-a-good-one/

Or watch a video that shows this same case study, using code *twtgift2016*: http://wholetruth.truthconcepts.com/maximize-your-real-estate-returns/.

Additionally, you can buy the working calculator for $200 at http://truthconcepts.com/buy-now/real-estate-analysis/.

ACKNOWLEDGMENTS

Kim

I'd like to thank Jimmy, my co-author, for coming up with the idea for this book and dedicating the time necessary to provide you an inside look at his work at Vreeland Capital. Additionally, I know his wife, Susie, contributed both by taking the pictures of his office wall where all the families are as well as keeping the kids at bay while he wrote or met with me and the Scribe Media team.

Speaking of which…everyone at Scribe Media was helpful, especially Nikki Katz, our Scribe. Additionally, Ted Flanagan, Amanda Ibey, Michael Nigen, Shannon Lee, Taryn Wood, Julianne Clancy, Diana Fitts, and Kelsey Adams for all their assistance.

Then, there is my team at www.Partners4Prosperity.com who keep things going while I write. Theresa Sheridan, Jill

Molitor, and Joe Jacubetz all play a critical role in helping clients buy and understand life insurance and the various alternative investments we work with.

We have an external team too that helps us look good out in the world where you see our work: Kate Phillips, David Jehlen, Mimi Klosterman, Gabe Mendoza, Terri Paley, Walter Hartford, Jason Rink, Carrie Putman, Jeune Taylor, and Spencer Shaw.

And most importantly, you the reader, many of which have read our other books and consume our blog and podcast materials consistently. We are all grateful to you!

Jimmy

I could never have undertaken writing a book like this without the support, love, and encouragement of my wife, Susie, and our four kids, Maria, Bubba, Tommy, and Johnny. They are why I wake up every morning and go do what I do. Susie's constant encouragement has kept me going and made this dream of writing a book possible.

I owe a huge debt of gratitude to my parents, Steve and Ann Vreeland. I also owe a huge debt to my brother Timmy and sister Katie. I have invested in houses with all of my family members, and they all are currently involved in my business at some capacity now. My parents also created an environment in our home growing up that encouraged constant reading and learning.

I also want to acknowledge my team at Vreeland Capital and STLRTO that do an incredible job running these businesses. I want to especially acknowledge Steve Strode who is a business warrior and who I could not have built these businesses without.

I also want to acknowledge my partners at Cash Flow Tactics, Ryan Lee and Brad Gibb. They are phenomenal business partners and have helped me get focused and grow.

I want to acknowledge all of my investors, lenders, and buyers who have believed in me and my visions for my business. I also owe a debt of gratitude to the Scribe Media team who helped me take my scattered ideas and collect them to make this book.

Finally, I would like to acknowledge Kim Butler and her husband, Todd Langford, who have been mentors in teaching me how personal and business finances should work and how I can build my wealth. They have also been mentors to me in building my business, and I am extremely grateful for their friendship.

ABOUT THE AUTHORS

Kim D. H. Butler and Jimmy Vreeland have decades of combined expertise in the real estate and life insurance industries. Kim is president of Partners for Prosperity, which offers clients financial help nationwide over the phone and web, and the cofounder of The Prosperity Economics Movement, which offers an alternative to "typical" financial planning. Jimmy created Vreeland Capital to capitalize on unique real estate opportunities. Drawing on years of experience, Vreeland Capital has secured more than one hundred distressed properties, often at just thirty to forty cents on the dollar.

Made in the USA
Coppell, TX
06 November 2019